Troikapocalypse

Rita Costa • Gary Dougall • Inês Costa

© 2012 Rita Costa, Gary Dougall, Inês Costa All Rights Reserved

ISBN 978-1-291-10512-4

First Edition September 2012

Special Thanks

Our mysterious benefactor
Our families for putting up with our silliness
Our friends
Andre Luis
Danielle Webber
Diana Teixeira
Duarte Rosado
Chad Hay
Giorgio Manes
Graham Stenhouse
Helena Ramos
Jalal Poehlman
Lewis Paine
Maria Paulouro Roque
Nuno Chambel

And to everyone who believed in us!

Contents

CONTENTS 5
1. WHAT'S ALL THIS ABOUT A CRISIS THEN? 7
2. WHY "TROIKAPOCALYPSE"? 13
3. A HISTORY OF THE CRISIS 16
4. THE STATE OF AFFAIRS 21
5. WHO DO WE BLAME? 31
6. WHO SHOULD YOU VOTE FOR? 41
7. SAVING MONEY 50
8. YAY! YOU'RE A GEEK! 63
9. HOW THE SUN KILLED OUR ECONOMY 67
10. PACK YOUR BAGS, LET'S EMIGRATE! 75
11. IS CRIME THE ANSWER? 84
12. ENTERTAINMENT 89
13. THE WONDERS OF ONLINE SHOPPING 102
14. INVESTMENTS 112
15. STUCK IN JOB PURGATORY? 120
16. PIMP YOUR LIFE 125
17. THE IDIOT'S GUIDE TO JOB HUNTING 147
18. HOW TO BECOME A MORTUARY AGENT 152
19. HOW TO BATTLE CRISIS DEPRESSION 156
20. A RECIPE FOR DISASTER 163
21. WHAT IF CIVILISATION WERE TO COLLAPSE? 177
22. IDEAS FOR SUPPLEMENTAL INCOME 186
23. PROCRASTINATION 193
24. TO CONCLUDE… 203
GLOSSARY 206

1. What's All This About A Crisis Then?

Unless you have been living in a cave, you know all about the financial difficulties that have gripped Europe, and much of the rest of the world, over the last few years. If you don't, then put the book down and venture out of the cave for a while.

Come back when you are done.

We're not experts on the subject, but we've lived through it, and have found that unless you are, listening to those trying to explain all this causes severe headaches. As such we are about to give you our less knowledgeable, yet non headache inducing, take on the situation.

The first piece of wisdom we have to impart is that even in this crisis, alternative funding methods like crowdfunding websites Kickstarter and Indiegogo are flourishing. In fact, Indiegogo helped make this book a reality.

Many of our friends rallied round to pre-order our book and help us get it off the ground. We'd like to thank everyone who has shown faith that we won't disappoint with the finished product. Buying a book before it is written is not the most traditional way of doing things, and we can't thank you enough for it!

1. What's All This About A Crisis Then?

While we don't think anyone's life will be changed by reading this, we don't think it's too presumptuous to say that we think there will be some helpful stuff in here for most people. Unfortunately we don't have all the answers. None of us can see the future, though Gary tries almost every day. We could be wrong about a lot of things, or just plain crazy.

You should decide for yourself what is best for you and what advice to take and what advice to ignore. Those of you with a fear of dead bodies should not seek employment in the funeral business for example, while those of you who are a few burgers away from a heart attack should not suddenly buy a treadmill, or your family will be the ones needing someone in the funeral business.

Dealing with money issues and career problems is always hard. We are not immune to these issues, but we believe we've collected a lot of common sense together, along with some complete nonsense, that will prove to be useful. Yes, even the nonsense.

We will lead with the obvious stuff. Don't eat yellow snow, don't poke sleeping bears with sticks and do not connect any of your body parts to a car battery. We'll get to the more specific stuff later.

If you live in Europe, you have suffered more than most during this crisis. Years of history, modernization, globalization and unity have come back to haunt you. And the worst bit? There is nothing you can do about it. Even if you are a responsible voting adult you are rowing against a tsunami of ignorance, laziness and overall indifference.

Don't get us wrong, there is still some hope in this world (insert your own cute photo of a baby playing with a puppy here), but it is heart wrenching to look around and see your family, friends and loved ones unemployed and packing their bags to try their luck elsewhere. It's one thing to dream of traveling and having international experiences, another is when you are given a one way ticket after college that is labelled "return somewhat richer in the distant future".

Modernisation has brought us many new technologies to keep in touch with people almost anywhere on the planet, but many of those technologies cost a lot of people their jobs, and have contributed to people needing to move to find work. You'll be able to easily keep in touch with your loved ones, but you will also miss many of the most important moments in each other's lives.

Let's try comparing two case studies.

Case 1: The Over-Qualified Studious "Idiot"

So you decide to study something like History or Political Science.

You study for at least twelve years before you enrol in college, study for 3 more years for a bachelor degree and then you go nuts and decide you want to complete your masters in the next two years. Because you are committed (or insane) you'll enrol full time which will make it close to

1. What's All This About A Crisis Then?

impossible to find a full time paying job. So depending on your luck and how successful your family is, you'll postpone earning any significant amount of money until you are at least 23 years old (and here we are assuming you are quite smart, you skip wild college parties and complete all your classes on your first attempt - which probably means that you are either a robot or an alien).

Assuming you find some kind of summer or part time job and/or your family continues to give you some sort of a spending allowance, you will probably save up a maximum of €500 a year from the age of eighteen.

So in 5 years you will have €2,500 in the bank, you will still live with your parents and, if you are lucky, you will probably own a car built in 1990 that still runs every day. Because you have a degree you will probably find a full time job earning you a maximum of €1,000 (after all, we are called the 1K Generation).

Congratulations, by the time you are 30 you will either still live with your parents or you will live in a rented flat with your significant other trying to survive and you cannot afford any special vacations anywhere. Your biggest achievement is being over-educated and underpaid.

Let's try to look at the opposite spectrum and another good example of our modern times.

Case 2: The "*You Will Never Accomplish Anything In Life*" Free Soul

Now imagine that you are eighteen, you finish high school

and you decide that, taking into account the unemployment rates, which are at an all-time high, you need to start working right away. Because you do not have a college degree, you will probably start lower down the corporate ladder, let's say, at a clothing shop. Depending on where you are in Europe, you will probably start earning around €800 a month, but because you still live with your parents, this means you can save probably as much as €400 a month. So €400 x 12 = €4,800 a year.

By the time you are twenty three you will have a potential €24,000 saved up which means you can buy your first car, start saving to own your own house and have money for going out, vacations and little luxuries.

Do you remember all those times your parents and teachers told you to study and get good grades if you wanted to succeed? Was that a lie? Well no, it wasn't. But they failed to mention that even with a good education, success was never guaranteed.

Often people doing skilled jobs like carpentry or plumbing can earn significantly more money than lawyers or architects. It's not all about the high prestige job. Keep in mind your child might never go to college, but it doesn't mean they can't do well for themselves.

Their dream of doing it Jesus-style and becoming a carpenter might not be that ridiculous. If they actually think they are Jesus, that's another matter altogether, unless they are convincing, in which case you should immediately start a cult to take advantage of the many fools out there looking for something crazy to believe in!

1. What's All This About A Crisis Then?

Just do whatever you want with your life but balance real life and expectations in order to avoid terrible disappointment and a miserable life where you wake up every single day wanting to die. Life is not supposed to be that hard. Unless you live in a Third World country and you are trying to figure out if you have enough money to feed your kids rice tomorrow, you are not doing too badly. You shouldn't take how easy your life is for granted and be appreciative of the opportunities your parents gave you for actually letting you study and not sending you to work in the fields to harvest potatoes and tomatoes.

2. Why "Troikapocalypse"?

This book is called Troikapocalypse, a combination of the words "Troika" and "Apocalypse". Are you confused? Don't worry, that's what we are here for, we will explain everything.

Troika...

The definition of "Troika" states that it is a collection of judges or political leaders. Culturally it was a "a sled or carriage drawn by three horses" but modern times have given it a completely new definition, those three horses being the International Monetary Fund, European Central Bank and European Commission trying to save Europe from certain Doom. This powerful triumvirate has taken the reigns (pun intended) of the situation in an attempt to deal with the crisis. They are trying to prevent countries like Greece, Ireland, Portugal, Spain and Italy from going bankrupt and bringing the Euro currency down with it.

According to Bloomberg, over €386 billion have been given to different European countries to try to prevent this economic Apocalypse from happening right now. First was Greece, in March 2010, followed by Ireland in November 2010. Portugal asked for a bailout in May 2011. Eurozone Finance Ministers established a bailout fund called the "European Stability Mechanism" to pay for all these bailouts.

2. Why "Troikapocalypse"?

Finally in May of 2012 Spain requested a bailout (more accurately the Spanish banks asked for loans), followed by Cyprus in June 2012, maybe proving that the Euro crisis may be contagious and not as contained as initially thought. The situation in Cyprus was caused to their banking sector and the amount of Greek debt they hold.

The Troika personnel are working hard in close proximity to local governments to figure out and implement measures to save those local economies. They have workgroups that accompany how that bailout money is spent and they come up with new measures to prevent new bailouts. Are they being successful? Well... Yes and no. The debt situation is being dealt with, but economies are being ravaged at the same time.

... Apocalypse

Are we being pessimistic by calling this an "Apocalypse"? It's the year 2012, how could we not use this opportunity to establish a comparison with Mayan predictions that the world would end in 2012? We, of course, know those predictions were loose interpretations of the Mayan calendar and that the Mayans probably never predicted such a thing, but if Hollywood gets to use this idea, so do we. After all, the Oxford Dictionary definition of "Apocalypse" states it's an *"event involving destruction or damage on an awesome or catastrophic scale"*. The Eurozone on the edge of collapse? We think that qualifies as something on a catastrophic scale.

After unifying most of Europe under a single currency, the

Troikapocalypse

Euro, Europe basically tied all its markets and economies together, but left the budgetary controls with all the member governments, leaving the whole area vulnerable to the problems of any of its members.

We are fairly surprised that emergency plans had to be created to try to help the EU out and that no one had drawn up plans detailing what to do should something like this ever happen. It's like a house of playing cards, and the bottom is not secure. It seems no one entertained the thought this was even possible.

We sincerely hope the whole thing doesn't come crashing down, because, hey, we live here, we like Europe and being able to pay for food and having a place to live. We hope this book helps you keep your head up and gives you some tips on getting a new job, keeping your old one or saving some money. We will not be giving you amazing tips on how to navigate the stock market and how to take advantage of this big mess, if we had them we would be using them ourselves and instead of writing this we could be in the Maldives drinking our fruity drinks and making fun of the other tourists with less money than us.

Alas life is cruel and there will be no lavish vacations this year. There will be watching the news more intently for signs that this Apocalypse is being fought by the powerful Troika and that they actually know what they are doing and are not making things up as they go along.

3. A History Of The Crisis

We really don't want to bore you but we have to give you a small history lesson about Europe and more specifically the European Union. Stop complaining, no need to start yawning; you haven't even started reading yet. Afterwards you can tell all your friends that you are super smart and know all sorts of random things that aren't useful in real life. When you are all arguing about salary cuts you can use random bits of information to make it seem like you actually read the newspapers every day.

The European Union

The European Union began in the 40s and 50s but not as we know it now. Winston Churchill first talked about a "United States of Europe" in 1946, seeking unity among the European countries. So in 1951 the European Steel and Coal Community was created, a first draft of what we know today as the EU, a pretty concept to try to prevent another major war, the first organization in the world based on the principles of supranationalism. After many treaties and other "Communities", in 1967 the Merger Treaty created the European Communities. From a small union of countries that only included France, Italy, the Benelux countries and West Germany, several other countries joined from this period up until the 80s, including Denmark, Ireland, the United Kingdom, Greece, Spain and

3. A History Of The Crisis

Portugal. Eventually the European Union was created, substituting the European Communities.

This union created a necessity of facilitating commerce and the exchange of goods and services amongst the member states. The creation of a Single Currency had been discussed since the 60s but it only came to fruition in 1993 with the Maastricht Treaty. All member states with the exception of the United Kingdom and Denmark joined the Euro. In 2002 coins and notes began to circulate. The Euro had arrived, with promises of economic stability, prosperity, ponies and ice-cream for everyone.

The states and countries that use the Euro nowadays as their currency are Austria, Belgium, the Netherlands, Finland, France, Germany, Ireland, Italy, Luxembourg, Monaco, Portugal, San Marino, Spain, the Vatican, Greece, Slovenia, Cyprus, Malta, Slovakia and Estonia.

Flash forward to 2008. After many years living under the illusion of prosperity, a new Great Depression started, much to the surprise of citizens everywhere. Since we are not writing a thesis on the entire world, we'll just talk about Europe. Europe is suffering through a sovereign debt crisis. What the hell is that? We were a little confused at first too.

The sovereign debt is what sovereign states (countries) owe to either national lenders (internal debt) or international lenders (external debt). Governments usually borrow money by issuing products like securities, government bonds or bills, to pay for their bills, since they keep spending more than they actually make. When a government cannot pay back its lenders, this is called a sovereign default. As governments have more and more difficulty in paying their debts, interest rates go up and it becomes harder and harder for governments to borrow more money and to repay back the money they already owe. It's a snowball effect. The more you owe the harder it becomes to pay it back, and your lenders, fearful of you not paying back your loans, speculate about this, making interest rates go up, and making you owe more and more. Basically you're screwed.

Why do certain European countries owe so much money to lenders? If we could answer this question we would be winning the Nobel Prize for Economics right about now. Mainly it is related to bad management of government money. For more details on this, consult our chapter "Who do we blame".

European Finance Ministers keep approving rescue packages to avoid states like Greece, Ireland and Portugal from going into default and for them to be able to repay their debts. Governments continue to spend money as if it grows on trees. Actual countries who don't have a massive debt know that someone will have to foot that dinner bill and that Greece has left the table just in time to go to the bathroom, crawl out a window and leave in a taxi. It's a mess. And you just know Portugal and Spain have conveniently left their wallets at home. Maybe they shouldn't have ordered the lobster.

The Euro

Does this mean the end of the Euro? Are weaker countries

3. A History Of The Crisis

dragging the others into the muck? Maybe. The Germans and the Dutch have manifested their apprehension over bailing out other countries who can't repay their debt.

The Euro might not collapse but there is a possibility that a few countries could go back to their national currencies. Can Greece afford to go back to the Drachma? Probably not. If this happens foreign investors will flee their investments in problem states as quickly as possible. Does anybody even remember currencies like the Portuguese Escudo, the Spanish Peseta or the Italian Lira? What would happen to those economies when faced with a harder time trading with other European countries (due to rising exchange costs), their currency being severely undervalued compared to the Euro? Can we afford to undo the work of ten years and just bring back those dead currencies?

Since we would no longer have a common currency, would that mean the death of the Schengen Agreement too? The Schengen Agreement allows for the movement of people and goods amongst European countries without crossing borders. Would this make any sense in a post-Euro era? Who knows, maybe, Ireland for example has the Euro but does not belong to the Schengen Agreement. The reverse situation could also work in theory, with countries having their own currency but their borders still open for anyone to come and go without any border control.

Maybe Europe has to move forward and instead of only having a monetary union, pushing to create a fiscal union as well, integrating economic policies and maybe removing a little autonomy from each country's government. This is

Troikapocalypse

a very touchy subject. Most countries would have a hard time dealing with the idea of losing political autonomy and accepting guidelines on such a deep level. This could lead to the loss of a country's national identity. Thinking back to Churchill's "United States of Europe". We all know how that went for the United States of America, a civil war...

We are speculating. If we had answers we would gladly share them, for a small fee of course. One thing we can agree with: Europe is in a crisis. Unemployment levels continue to increase as well as costs and taxes. Small businesses, especially restaurants, are closing down. The poor are getting poorer. Newspapers and magazine articles are comparing this to the Great Depression of the 1930s, and if that doesn't scare you we don't know what will.

We don't want to think about people starving to death or holding signs saying "will work for food" in front of local stock exchanges. We still hold out hope for everything to work out and for us to continue to afford our bourgeois lifestyle. Our generation, born after the 1970s, never suffered through a Great War or a big crisis. We are spoiled and we have never had, and are not prepared to, face hardship, hunger or war.

We hope that in 2013 or 2014 our biggest concern will be where to park our hovercrafts and how come there's such a long line for the teleportation chamber. We are the Me Generation. We were raised to believe that a college degree would open all doors for us.

Unfortunately for many of us the only doors opened right now are at the Unemployment Office.

4. The State Of Affairs

Let's recap some of the important events that have brought us to where we are right now in 2012.

A History Lesson, AGAIN

The first indicator of serious economic problems in Europe was on August 9th 2007. French bank *BNP Paribas* froze three of its funds, claiming it had no way to value them. These funds were made up of subprime loans. It was the first major bank to come out and say there was a serious issue brewing with these loans. This date has been compared to August 4 1914, a change from a prosperous time for banks, to an all out trench warfare. A fight for survival.

A month later on September 14th, *Northern Rock* bank in the UK, due to a decrease in demand for securitised mortgages, found itself needing a loan from the UK government. Panic quickly ensued as people feared the bank would go bankrupt and suddenly everyone and their dog wanted their money withdrawn immediately. This was the first run on a British bank in 150 years.

On the 17th of February 2008, the UK government nationalised Northern Rock as a "temporary measure".

On the 17th of September 2008 the UK's biggest mortgage

4. The State Of Affairs

lender, HBOS, had to be rescued by Lloyds TSB in a £12 billion deal after a run on HBOS shares. Alex Salmond, (now first minister of Scotland) said at the time "*I am very angry that we can have a situation where a bank can be forced into a merger by basically a bunch of short-selling spivs and speculators in the financial markets. All financial regulators have got to wake up to where we are at the present moment*".

September 30th 2008 saw the Irish government guarantee all deposits in the country's main banks for 2 years, a decision that would soon come back to haunt them. Just a week later Iceland's three main banks collapsed and had to be nationalised. To protect British customers' the UK government froze the assets of their UK subsidiaries. The fact they used anti-terror laws to do this should concern you, since we always hear about how these Draconian laws cannot be used for other things.

Less than a week later, on the 13th of October, the UK government gave RBS, HBOS and Lloyds TSB a £37 billion rescue package to prevent a similar collapse in the UK banking system. Paul Myners, the UK financial services Secretary said "*RBS, HBOS and Lloyds were experiencing a professional bank run, where the markets were no longer willing to fund the UK banks. That's why we stepped in. We will never appreciate how close we came to a collapse of the banking system.*"

November 20th 2008 was the date of the first European Governmental bailout. The International Monetary Fund loaned $2.1 billion to Iceland. This was the first time since 1976 that a Western European nation had needed a loan from the IMF. Due to Iceland's size, the small value of the loan and the fact Iceland is not part of the Eurozone; this was a relatively contained event.

The year 2009 saw the G20 introduce a global stimulus package of $5 trillion in an attempt to save the global economy from sinking. The still worsening situation in Europe came to a head on April 27th 2010 when Greek debt was downgraded to "junk". Five days later, the 2nd of May, signalled the start of the main Eurozone crisis. Greece, having finally got Germany on board by promising to enact severe austerity measures, became the first Eurozone nation to be bailed out by the Troika.

A series of loans totalling €110 billion were approved to prevent the Greeks from defaulting on their debt. Their system of tax evasion and bribes had finally been exposed as not being the best fiscal governance.

On November 28th 2010, with economies imploding all over Europe, Ireland was the next nation to need a bailout. €67.5 billion was necessary. Similar to what Greece had experienced, protests over the austerity measures were widespread. The Irish government would see their support collapse in the next election. The fact that it was the banks and the banks alone that made this bailout necessary was ignored as the government took the blame.

On May 5th 2011, Portugal became the next nation to receive a bailout when a package was agreed to provide them up to €78 billion worth of loans. Unlike Greece, Portugal wasn't known for engaging in tax evasion as a national sport. Citizens were shocked but accepted the

4. The State Of Affairs

severe austerity measures that were immediately put in place. They did not head to the streets with Molotov cocktails and an angry attitude. No riots took place.

By July 21st 2011, the Greeks, having completely failed to get their act together, had to be given a second bailout of €130 billion. More austerity measures were met by more protests and a sharp decline in the country's GDP.

Portugal

As of the middle of 2012, Europe is still in turmoil. Portugal is paradoxically described as doing very well, and very badly. The Troika is delighted with Portugal, as their austerity measures mean they are on target to reduce their deficit by the promised amount by the promised time. Unfortunately they don't take into account the human cost of this.

Public sector wages were slashed by up to 25%, in some cases even more. Taxes were raised. Any hope of anyone getting a pay rise anytime soon evaporated like a snowflake in the oven.

Fuel taxes are up too, with gasoline now costing the equivalent of $8 a gallon. If you don't even know what a gallon is, that is more than double the cost in America where many are complaining that it is too expensive.

Bonuses were taken away and the cost of healthcare has more than doubled in some cases. A trip to the emergency room that was €9 in 2011 was upped to €20. This might not sound like a lot to Americans, but in Europe where universal health care is widespread, an increase of over 120% is unprecedented. Non-governmental organisations say that the poor and elderly in Portugal can no longer afford essential care.

There have been reports of people stopping taking medication as they do not have money for extravagances such as food, never mind medicine. Free transport services to get people to hospitals have been suspended. These types of cuts always hit the poorest first, and while the government denies any connection, the month after health care prices were hiked and the free transport became a paid service, Portugal's death rate spiked by 20%. And we are not even taking into consideration the impact on criminality and its consequences.

Portugal is still deep in recession and the recovery process is likely to be lengthy. The unemployment rate reached 15.4% as of May 2012. The Portuguese people are paying a heavy price so their government can be the Troika's poster child. Portugal will get their debt under control, but their economy and people will have been ravaged by the process.

Greece

It appears that while Portugal is the favoured child, Greece is the one with ADHD who won't take its meds and Spain is the one hiding under the table trying not to get noticed after being naughty. In the end everyone is going to get grounded and sent to bed without supper.

Greece, you see, is apparently full of tax dodgers and criminals. While tax evasion is more common in southern

4. The State Of Affairs

Europe than up north, the Greeks are the European champions. Around €20 billion is lost in unpaid taxes every year. Considering the small size of the Greek economy, that's a massive amount of cash.

You might wonder why the Greek government doesn't crack down on this. They do try, but the problem appears to be that many officials are corrupt. The Greeks engage in a practice called *"Fakelaki"*. The word itself means *"little envelope"*, and the Greeks use this in the way many of us use the word *"tip"*. Unlike with a tip though, this is not given for a job well done, this is given to get the job done at all, or in the case of tax officials, so they don't need to pay taxes. A €3,000 tax bill turns into a €1,000 fakelaki to the taxman and both are happy. This is helping the country's economy collapse in on itself.

Have you seen the Harry Potter films? You know the scene where envelopes are flying all over the offices like flocks of birds? Well that's what it is like in Greece, except the envelopes don't actually fly, they are handed over, and they are full of money, but you get the idea. We are sorry for being so straightforward about the Greek, we aren't saying all of you are corrupt, but people did take advantage of the system. Many honest people are paying for the mistakes of a large group of petty criminals.

Money is handed over, among other reasons, to get better appointments, to make sure your planning application gets dealt with this decade and to keep transactions in cash, making them cheaper and denying the government tax revenue both from the value added tax that would be chargeable on the transaction, as well as the income that goes unreported.

The London Business School said in a paper that the Greek tax system was broken and that the current tax authority was *"beyond salvation."* They also made note of the fact that senior officials at the ministry of finance had predicted *"astonishingly, that even if all the tax-collecting authorities were shut down, state revenues would not suffer noticeably."*

Greece needs more help than the Troika can provide to get its house in order. It needs the populace to stop being tax evaders who are both giving and receiving bribes.

Ireland

Ireland is a different matter from Portugal and Greece. Its bailout wasn't made necessary by chronic governmental overspending. A property bubble burst in 2007, leaving banks exposed to high levels of debt from bankrupt construction companies and homeowners who couldn't afford to pay their mortgage.

The Irish government stepped in to guarantee the balances of all the people who had accounts with the banks in trouble. They also made sure investors who had bought bonds were protected. This was a noble attempt to shore up the banking sector and make sure no one lost their money. But when the effects of the global crisis hit, this resulted in the government being on the hook for far more money than they had ever expected.

4. The State Of Affairs

As a result of these bank guarantees, unemployment rose from 4% in 2006 to 14% in 2010. The Irish budget went from a surplus in 2007 to a deficit of 32% of GDP in 2010. This is the highest deficit ever registered in the European Union, and occurred while austerity measures were in effect. Bad timing is what screwed over Ireland, not bad management.

It is not all bad news though. Ireland is already receiving loans with lower interest rates and while it will be awhile before their economy fully recovers, there is little doubt that it is slowly happening.

Italy And Spain

No nation in Europe has been left untouched by the crisis; Italy and Spain in particular have been of concern, with Spain receiving loans of up to €100 billion, not for the government, but for its banks. Whether this is a bailout in the same way as those provided to other nations is a matter of debate. The money was lent directly to the banks, which means the extra debt will not put further pressure on the Spanish government's sovereign debt.

If you visit Spain the crisis is more visible than you think. Due to a property bubble, cities and suburbs are riddled with empty apartment blocks while financial districts are filled with shiny new glass towers.

The main problem with Spain is that it is considered "*too big to bail, too big to fail*". Why? Spain is home to 47 million people and has a $1.4 Trillion economy that was,

Troikapocalypse

until very recently, the Eurozone's fourth richest - after Germany, France and Italy. Spain alone was responsible for up around 11% of Europe's GDP. Try to visualize that Greece, Portugal and Ireland, the three Eurozone countries which have already received financial assistance, combined, make up less than 6% of Europe's economy. Now compare that number with Spain. Scared yet? We are.

Italy is also in a precarious position, but since they invented Pizza and Pasta, it means that even in a crisis, they can still eat wonderful food whilst the rest of Europe is feeding its children tuna sandwiches for dinner.

The Overall Picture

By August 2012, the feeling in most places is that barring any further catastrophes, local economies have started to heal, even though the improvement is likely to be a slow process. The one exception is Greece, where rumours of a third bailout persist, and the likelihood is one will be needed before this is over. Six-day work weeks are being considered. Of course, if this happens, the shit could really hit the fan and, depending on the reaction of the Greek public, everyone in Europe could get spattered.

Unlike countries like Japan, Europeans are not used to working more to try to improve their economy. This notion of self-sacrifice was never needed before, even after two world wars. If you ask citizens to give up an extra day of

4. The State Of Affairs

their week to pay debts they did not create themselves, expect more dissatisfaction and riots.

We now have to play the waiting game and see if austerity measures are indeed having a positive effect in the long run or if they are just life support for an already terminal patient.

5. Who Do We Blame?

It is human nature to want to assign blame. Whenever anything goes wrong, there is almost always someone or something at fault, and that is where the blame should land. Unfortunately it is also human nature to be wrong. Often incredibly, spectacularly, insanely, nowhere at all near the mark, wrong.

So, Who Do We Blame For All This?

What caused such a global collapse? The answer is fairly straightforward, the blame belongs to America. Due to their position as the world's biggest economy, any difficulties of the scale they experienced, starting in 2007, quickly spread like a cancer throughout the world. To show how badly the American economy was hit, in October 2007, the Dow Jones average was over 14,000 points. By March 2009, it was 6,600 points. You don't need to know anything about the economy to know that if it has fallen to less than half of that previous high, that can't be good at all.

Now having said that, it would be unfair to put all the blame on America. Yes, they started it, without them it probably wouldn't have happened at all. But it would be unfair not to mention that there's still a pretty decent chunk of blame that can be chopped up and handed out in

5. Who Do We Blame?

little bits to all those who contributed to the current state of affairs.

We could attribute some of the blame to those involved in the creation of the Euro. Trying to synchronise currency over so many nations, but with no harmonisation of the budget process was at best naive wishful thinking. At worst, totally crazy. There should also be some issued to all the construction companies around the world, who while seemingly lacking a basic understanding of economics, or, you know, good sense, saw a sharp increase in house prices, then decided it would be a good idea to borrow huge amounts of money to flood the market with even more real estate. A marvellous plan, until the prices inevitably came down and everyone lost all their money.

Individual governments don't escape here, many of them building up massive debts that weren't exactly good fiscal policy before the crisis kicked in. At least some of the blame needs to lie in those who overspent in good times, leaving themselves increasingly vulnerable in the bad times.

Let's not forget the rating agencies. Their decisions on what ratings a country gets have a direct effect on how much interest they need to pay on new bonds. Rather suspiciously, many of the downgrades during the European Sovereign Debt Crisis occurred just before major summits, leading many to suspect they had their own agendas. Their power over entire governments should be feared. They can topple regimes with a single downgrade.

We could go on all day like this, but instead we will analyse some of the more fringe theories of what can affect the economy. Maybe we have all overlooked some really obvious problems that could have easily been resolved before.

Clench

First off we have the part of the economy most familiar to most people. Retail. We all go shopping and the majority of us, once we enter the shop, turn into magpies. As we go to get the three things we came in for, the reaction of "ooo, shiny" often has the small basket, which was more than sufficient for the 3 things we needed, overflowing by the time we get near the cashiers.

According to Aparna A. Labroo at the University of Chicago and Iris W. Hung at the National University of Singapore, published in the Journal for Consumer Research, you should firm your muscles to avoid spending extra money, for example by making a fist. This can provide the extra willpower to leave those unneeded things on the shelf. So, apparently all you need to do to stop buying all that junk is to clench. Continually. In the shop. Though only if you have a goal and you really want to achieve it.

Hmmm.

Your task for the next week. Clench. Now which muscle, or indeed muscles, you decide to clench, is completely up to you. You never know, it may just make a difference to your finances. It also may be a complete waste of time. Either way, you are likely to look like a fool in the shop!

5. Who Do We Blame?

Next up is religion. Sort of.

Jesus Is Coming. Look Busy

A couple of Harvard researchers, Robert Barro & Rachel McCleary, looking at decades of data from fifty nine countries, concluded that populations with a large number of people who believe in Hell had more prosperous economies and suffered less corruption than the rest. We are going to go out on a limb and assume not many of these 59 countries were in Africa.

The effect seems specific to belief in Hell. Believing in a God did not make all that much of a difference, but the thought of Eternal Damnation was enough to keep more people honest. It is unknown if they took into account that countries where they believe in Hell are likely to be countries with a large concentration of Christians, which often points to Western nations, which typically do better anyway. Much of Africa is also a Christian stronghold, but we could not find anyone willing to say they had data showing fear of Hell prevented corruption there.

Are you a God botherer? Have you been stopped from cheating people by your fear of being condemned to Hell for all eternity? Or are you like us, and fear prison more than a fiery netherworld?

The answer may be very simple. People in Western civilization have a better grasp from watching television and movies that their frail physique would not allow them to survive very well in captivity. A person who thinks going through hardship is having to wait an extra week for their video games to come in the mail is not prepared to trade cigarettes to avoid being beat up on a weekly basis.

Those who are confident in their despicability are a whole different animal. Read on.

Killing In The Name Of-

Another reason you may not be doing as well financially as you had hoped, is that you are not a psychopath.

Psychopaths, like everything else, come in many flavours. They are not all out there committing all manner of terrible crimes. Some of them, many of them in fact, are doing well for themselves in business, banking, etc. usually at the expense of others.

Professor Robert Hare of the University of British Columbia, an expert in psychopaths, says that corporate psychopaths are *"ruthless, manipulative, superficially charming and impulsive"*. Ironically these traits are more than likely the ones companies look for in people they want in leadership positions. Anything to further the goals of the company.

Wall Street is said to be one of the main places they can be found, drawn to the money and power they can acquire there. You see, being the nice guy is why you are not rich. Being the bad guy is likely to pay off, as long as you are not concerned about whom you need to screw over to get there.

5. Who Do We Blame?

Talking about screwing people over, in an economic sense, it is not always easy to spot when this is happening. Take, as a fine example, the illegal downloading of music. A study conducted by Ipsos Mori, found that those who were illegally downloading music, actually spent more on music than those who didn't. Other studies have shown similar results in relation to both films and video games. The entertainment industry would have you believe piracy costs them huge, immense amounts of revenue. Unfortunately no one who does not work for them has been able to produce anything at all to support this. Illegal downloaders may be the ones who end up going to the cinema more often, buy more music on iTunes and generate publicity for relatively unknown bands, movies or artists. They are better informed.

If you want a better understanding of the crazy lies these industries tell, search for a video on YouTube called "the 8 billion iPod". It's a TED talk by comic author Rob Reid which gets to the heart of the issue of how much the creative industries are damaged by piracy.

Those Pesky Scientists

When not being lied to by the RIAA, we need to watch out for scientists too. Money that could be used to help real people is being squandered as it seems governments are rather indiscriminate when trying to stimulate the economy.

In America, the federal government has perfected the art of spending money on truly ludicrous things. Of the $787 billion handed out in the stimulus package, rather than target it well towards things that would actually help people, they funded a lot of studies that can only be described as completely ludicrous.

Here are a few examples of this.

In Atlanta, Georgia, an assistant professor at Georgia Tech managed to get himself $762,372 to study improvised music. Now to be clear, this is music that they come up with at the time, a jam session if you will. He found a way to receive funds so he could jam with *"world-renowned musicians"*. It was also claimed they would use brain imaging to understand the creative process. We've seen many medical dramas, and we are fairly sure that the machines they use for brain imaging don't have space inside them for instruments, though we do hope to one day find video evidence of what happened when they turned on the MRI while someone was in it with a triangle. We also need to point out that all music started off as improvisation.

Staying in Atlanta, Georgia State University was given $677,462 to study monkey and chimpanzee responses to inequality.

We'll just pause for a second while you take that in.

An extract from the grant application states - *"Seven species of primates will be asked to make decisions about whether or not to accept rewards in a series of studies in which their outcomes vary relative to their social partners. The influence of social factors like group*

5. Who Do We Blame?

membership and individual factors like personality will also be investigated. The results of this research will clarify how decision-making is affected by unequal outcomes." The real kicker here is that they have actually done this research before. The results were that chimpanzees were temperamental when they didn't get what they wanted and neither species reacted well to inequality. We can only surmise they want to do it again to rule out the possibility that the first batch of faeces throwers were all just mean assholes.

Next on the list is the Southwest Research Institute (SWRI) in Texas. They inexplicably managed to secure $298,543 to provide weather forecasts. On other planets. They made the claim that *"The atmospheric forecasting of weather and climate on other planets has great public appeal"*. Exactly what they were smoking when they made this claim is not recorded.

Moving to North Carolina, the apparently mad scientists at Wake Forest University were given $144,541 to spend on cocaine to give to monkeys. Because, apparently they were unsure if monkeys, if given the choice, would take a load of cocaine. We would love to see the video of these scientists in white lab coats trying to buy $144,541 worth of cocaine from a drug dealer trying to convince him that it was for "research purposes". We are sure that the drug dealer in question still tells the story to his grandchildren about the time he participated in a scientific study. Videos of monkeys coked out of their faces would also be welcome.

Onto California, where the California Academy of Sciences was given $1.9 million so they could send some researchers to islands in the south western Indian Ocean and East Africa. Once there, these researchers were to capture, photograph and study, wait for it, over 3.000 different species of ants. These researchers were of opinion that this would be of interest to people. They were then to take all this info and put it on *AntWeb*. A website 100% dedicated to ants. You're probably thinking we are just screwing with you at this point. Grab something with an internet connection. Go to www.antweb.org and behold exactly what that $1.9 million bought.

Back to North Carolina for a minute, where the North Carolina State University Insect Museum, which has average annual visitor numbers of 44 people (less than 1 per week), were given $253,123 to start a feature on their website called "Insect Of The Week" and create and sell baseball-style insect trading cards. They also used this money to buy computer equipment and furniture. We are fairly sure they will also have bought fancy new display cases to show the world (or at least the 44 people who visit every year) their amazing trading cards.

Florida gets in on the act with the Florida International University getting $59,845 to analyse *"an explosion of lawsuits in 17th century Peru & Mexico"*. The University of Florida got $934,498 to study the DNA of lice, in an attempt to understand human evolution and migration.

Really.

Another study worth mentioning was the investment of $294,958 in "Reducing Menopausal Hot Flashes Through Yoga". Researchers at Wake Forest University wanted to

5. Who Do We Blame?

study whether Integral Yoga could be "*an effective method to reduce the frequency and/or severity of hot flashes*" in menopausal women. We got a hot flash just by reading this. Maybe we should participate in the study? Gary would like to point out this study is unlikely to have any benefits for him.

Are you wondering what $500,000 could buy? How about your own blue, 96-gallon, microchip-embedded recycling bin? Yes, the residents of Dayton, Ohio, were encouraged to recycle more by being tracked through their own radio frequency tracker blue bin. This might be a worthy investment if there was a small robot arm with a camera that would examine items, and any that were not for recycling would be thrown back at you with a speaker informing you that you were a "moron".

Finally, and most awesomely, the Embry-Riddle Aeronautical University in Daytona Beach was awarded $80,000 so that students can use a laser interferometer gravitational-wave observatory, Which Scotty must have beamed down from the Enterprise, "*with the goal of detecting tiny perturbations in the geometry of space-time*".

Admit it, now you're concerned space-time might be perturbed.

So who do we blame? There is a case to be made for it being no one's fault, and for it being everyone's fault. Or anything in between. Since blame isn't really going to help anyone at this point, we should maybe think more about how to survive it.

6. Who Should You Vote For?

If you live in one of the struggling European nations, we bet you are incredibly annoyed by your government. The sovereign debt keeps increasing, taxes keep going up, unemployment keeps rising, people keep getting poorer. The belief that all politicians are incompetent seems to be backed up by hard evidence.

So if all politicians are incompetent, who do you vote for? Is there such a thing as an honest trustworthy politician? Or a political party that will defend your best interests instead of its own?

When people are dissatisfied they tend to blame who they can, and the people running the country are the easiest and most common targets. It makes sense. People do have a short memory though. They forget that a crisis like this didn't come about due to just the actions of their own government. They also forget that economic effects are often very slow, and the trouble you find yourself in may have been generated by policies implemented years or decades ago.

The crisis in Greece is not just financial, it is political. The voters want someone to blame, and they have gone with the tried and true answer of "the politicians." After the

6. Who Should You Vote For?

May 2012 election, no party had a majority, and disagreement among all the parties as to which crazy idea was less crazy than all the others meant they were unable to form a coalition government either. After all attempts to form a government failed, new elections had to be called.

You see, when people become truly fed up with the mainstream political parties, you know, the ones who get more than a tiny amount of votes, they turn to the more fringe parties. Some are harmless and others are not. You know the type, the ones with white hoods, or skinheads with a massive amount of tattoos. Maybe pitchforks or Molotov cocktails too.

We are not saying you should determine who is the most boring and vote for them just because you are too afraid of the alternatives. But you shouldn't just give up on the whole process like many do. If you didn't vote, you have no one to blame but yourself if you end up with a bunch of xenophobic idiots ruining your country instead of just normal idiots. When people who think being a xenophobe is a bad idea stop voting, the lunatics who disagree are able to punch well above their weight.

Just because that other party will cut those taxes that will make you a whole €50 a year better off, stop and think about whether they make sense, or if it seems like while you'll have an extra €50, the economy on the whole will implode leaving you with no job the next year due to your employer going bust.

Remember that politicians have specific jobs, and while they are happy to claim credit for everything up to and including the rising of the sun in the morning, the reality is they actually have control over very little. The President of the United States of America hasn't been able to pass a budget in three years as of the time of writing due to the craziness of the internal politics in America, yet he is still referred to as the world's most powerful man.

Don't get caught up in the media storm that occurs almost every time there is a hint that a politician might have gotten something wrong. The idea that if there is a scandal involving one of them, then their entire party also must be responsible is ludicrous, yet common.

A More Practical Example

Imagine the situation as if it was happening in your workplace. If there is a guy in the IT department downloading songs illegally, and there almost certainly *is* a guy in your IT department who is downloading songs illegally, then does that mean they need to shut the whole company down? Make your own decisions; don't just choose between the options offered by the media.

Conversely, you should probably stop electing thieves and assholes to office. If they seem skeevy and act dodgy, if they are known for not being honest, maybe they are not the best candidate. The logic behind this being as advanced as the logic of "*if it looks like a duck, and quacks like a duck, well...*"

If you are unhappy with your current government go to the public demonstrations and do so peacefully. And do go out and vote when the time comes, don't whine about it later

6. Who Should You Vote For?

and say that you didn't vote but if you had voted that guy would be the last on your list. That makes you part of the problem, not the solution.

Do not, and we repeat, do not, elect fundamentalist or radical parties because you think they will "stir things up". Yes they will. A few countries have tried that and it never went well. We know parties with strong crazy ideologies sometimes can draw you in because they appeal to your patriotic side, but these fringe ideas are dangerous.

Who are we to tell you who to vote for anyway? Just make your vote count.

How Not To Be Like Greece

In June 2012 Greece had a second legislative election in just over six weeks after no single party won an outright victory in the first poll. A complete inability to form a coalition government after almost 2 weeks of negotiation left no other option but for a new election to be called.

These elections were incredibly important for Greece. A pro-austerity government would take steps needed to ensure the payment of the bailouts next stage. This would prevent the complete collapse of their economy, not to mention the effects that would have on the Euro.

The alternative option was to vote for parties who were opposed to the austerity. Quite why this was ever a serious option for anyone who didn't yearn to suddenly live in a third world country is completely beyond us. We can't see how this could possibly have ended in anything except complete and utter disaster.

The people had to choose between two great options. Painful, but necessary austerity so they could get out of the hole they had found themselves in, or the batshit crazy option of continuing to spend all the money they didn't have until the country collapsed. Which would have probably been in less than a week. Unfortunately the people couldn't make up their minds any better than the government and they spread the vote in such a way no one was anywhere near the needed majority and the parties were unable to agree on the wetness of water, never mind what should be done about everything, so yeah. A second election.

The results were not tremendously different from the previous poll, but were different enough to mean they were able to put a coalition together to pass the austerity measures that would enable the bailout payments to continue.

While you are congratulating the Greeks for getting over their indecision, probably while doing the slow clap, keep in mind this probably saved much of Europe from sinking into what would probably have been a far worse depression than they were starting to come out of. The Greeks really did save the bacon of many when they decided to continue the austerity measures.

Fortunately cuts and tax raises haven't been as severe and reactions to them correspondingly smaller elsewhere.

6. Who Should You Vote For?

People have accepted them far more easily, albeit having suffered less.

How not to be like the Greek? Make up your mind and just choose somebody, anybody, to lead your country from the precipice and nearer to the light.

Oh, we should point out that violent opposition and activities such as setting fire to government buildings is probably not a good idea, due to the likelihood you will end up in jail. We will have more to say on crime later.

And The French?

The defeat of Nicolas Sarkozy in the May 2012 election is another example of a politician being blamed for something beyond their control. Unhappiness with unemployment and the economy had seen Sarkozy trail in the opinion polls, and ultimately led to his defeat, but considering the crisis that had gripped not just Europe, but much of the world; it's hard to see how France could have fared any better.

Sarkozy's successor, François Hollande, is a French socialist who ran on a platform of stimulating economic growth while returning to a balanced budget by 2017. He has outlined several ways he intends to raise money, along with several ways he intends to spend money. The specifics are available online, unfortunately in excruciating detail, but are of course less important to people than whether or not he does what he said he would. When was the last time a politician managed that?

While Sarkozy had wanted to decrease immigration and had threatened to leave the Schengen Agreement unless it was changed to allow stricter border controls, Hollande is a bigger fan of integration, seeking to draw up a new Franco-German partnership that will see the creation of a joint Franco-German military headquarters.

He is also pushing for more involvement in important EU decisions, saying he wants to give Europe a "new direction." Despite all the problems Europe has endured, the French people have voted for more integration, not less.

What About Other Countries?

Germany will have federal elections in 2013, along with Italy and The Netherlands. Most political analysts believe these elections will be focused more on Europe and holding it together rather than national problems. Further integration might prevent Europe from facing other situations similar to Greece's.

Italian Prime Minister Mario Monti has spoken of the *"psychological disintegration of Europe"*, indicating that Southern European nations, which have certainly fared worse than the Northern nations, were not happy with the benefits of being members of the European Union. One specific item mentioned was the cost of bonds, Monti believing the high rates his own government has to pay are subsidising the lower rates Germany gets.

Mario Monti, an economist, it would appear, knows

6. Who Should You Vote For?

nothing of economics. Considering he was not exactly elected as much as he was appointed after Berlusconi experienced scandal number 726 and resigned, it will be interesting to see if his strategy of "blame the Germans" gains any traction with the voters.

The Italian paper *Il Libero* ran a front page photo of Angela Merkel with the headline "The Fourth Reich". You can imagine where this is going.

With differing messages such as these coming from governments, it is hard to say how it will all end up, but it is clear many are not ready to come closer together, while others actively push for it.

Merkel has provided some humour too. Her image as being the strong woman of German and European politics has seen a sharp increase in the sending of the following email, often said to be a plan of Merkel's. The truth is it has been doing the rounds for longer than anyone can remember.

New EU Language Regulations

"The European Commission has just announced an agreement has been reached to use English in all internal dealings, rather than German, which was the other language under consideration. As part of the negotiations, Her Majesty's Government has accepted English could do with some improvement and a 5 year plan will be enacted to transition to the new Euro-English.

In the first year, "s" will replace the soft "c". Sertainly this will make sivil servants happy. The hard "c" will be dropped in favour of "k". This should klear up any konfusion and keyboards kan have one less letter on them.

There will be growing publik enthusiasm in the sekond year, when the troublesome "ph" will be replaced with "f". This makes the word fotograf 20% shorter!

By the third year, publik akseptanse of the new spelling kan be expekted to reach the stage where more komplikated changes are possible. double leters, which have always ben a deterent to akurate speling, wil be removed. Also al wil agre that the horible mes of the silent "e" in the languag is disgrasful and they should go away.

By the fourz year, peopl vil be reseptiv to steps such as replasing "th" with "z" and "w" with "v". During ze fifz year, ze unesesary "o" kan be dropd from vords kontaining "ou" and similar changes vud of kors be aplied to ozer kombinations of leters.

After zis fifz year, ve vil hav a realy sensibl riten styl. zer vil be no mor trubls or difikultis and evrivun vil find it ezi to understand each ozer.

ZE DREAM VIL FINALI KUM TRU!"

7. Saving Money

With prices increasing and your disposable income decreasing due to inflation and more bills, sooner or later you are going to have to decide to cut expenses and start saving money in case of an emergency. Nobody really likes it, money is for spending and not for keeping under the mattress, but it is better to be safe than sorry.

Learning where to save might be a very simple exercise in planning where your money is going and seeing what corners you can cut. Buying a new car every year for example, might not be the best idea ever.

Expenses

Sit down and make a list of fixed expenses you have every month. Electricity bill, water, gas, cell phone, internet, phone, digital television account, insurances, kids' school and loans. We won't talk about food in this chapter; you can save a lot of money on meals, just read the chapter "Recipes for the Crisis".

First, most people don't do this, but they should. Companies keep launching new products and lowering prices for their older products to attract new customers. Most cellphone and digital TV services companies do this, as well as internet service providers. They will not update their current customers' accounts though. So make a spread sheet with everything you pay monthly and then

7. Saving Money

visit every 6 months or so all those companies' websites and check how much they are charging for the services you are using. If they lowered their prices, then that is what customer support hotlines are for. Call and complain about it. Yes, you want to be that stingy caller. Most companies will not hesitate to lower the price to keep you, the loyal customer, happy.

Saving is basically being organized about where you spend your money and knowing what corners you can cut. Excel spread sheets are geeky, yes, but they will help you in the long run. Do you know how much you spend monthly? You should.

Most supermarkets nowadays have their own brand products which are much cheaper. Buy those products. All tomato sauce tastes the same. Your supermarket bill will lower a little bit. Cleaning products for your household, like window cleaner spray, are all the same really. You are not buying perfume, people; you are trying to save some pocket change. Condoms however are not all the same so please only cut corners where it is safe. A "faulty" ladder on sale? We wouldn't buy that, you shouldn't either. If you did buy those discount condoms before reading this paragraph, congratulations on being a mommy/daddy, we need a higher birth rate in developed countries with an ageing population so we salute you!

Gas Prices

This depends on the country of course but gas prices keep going up and a lot of people spend a fortune in gas driving to and from work. We have tried those "discount" gas stations where they're associated with supermarkets and have lower prices. Are they worth it? Not particularly. We have seen people wait hours in lines to fill up their tank in those gas stations. Why? Pay attention, this is important:

Time Is Money

You waiting in line for two hours means you are not doing something else a lot more productive for two hours. You are wasting hours of your precious life waiting in line to save a few cents while you could be home curing cancer or inventing a teleporter. And teleporters are so cool they need to be invented as soon as possible.

Ok, onwards to other places you can save money. Do you need to eat out that often? OK, your economy needs it or else restaurants will all go under, but do it less often. Cooking at home is not that bad. You could cook a feast for a tenth of the price in those two hours you wasted looking like an idiot at the gas station.

Traveling

Do you want to save money while traveling? Budget hotels and low cost airlines look like a great deal but you need to analyse everything before booking. Why?

Low Cost Airlines sound amazing, taking you to cities you always wanted to visit with good discounts if you compare them with other more "classical airlines". But be suspicious. First, luggage. Are you checking in any luggage? Most discount airlines will charge extra for those. Both ways. So add that to your initial ticket cost. Also most

7. Saving Money

low cost airlines will fly you to airports that are not as central as that city's main airports. So when you get to your destination you either need to waste a lot of hours in public transportations or you need to catch a very expensive taxi to your hotel. For example, Luton Airport is used by mainly low cost airlines and it is an hour from the centre of London, either by expensive train or slightly less expensive buses. Heathrow is much more convenient, being directly connected to the London underground.

Uh, Time To Do Math Again!

Low Cost Airline Ticket + Buses/Taxis + Charge for Hold Luggage + The Extra Time You Wasted Saving A Couple Of Euros = just buy that slightly more expensive airline ticket and stop trying to save just a handful of euros.

Hotels suffer from this same syndrome. People book hotels due to their amazing prices or discounts but they forget to check the hotel location. Great, you saved 20 dollars per evening booking at that cheaper hotel nearer to LAX on your California trip. How long does it take you to reach the tourists attractions you wanted to visit? At least one hour each way? Not worth it. Do you remember what we told you before? Time is Money.

You need to find the perfect balance between saving money and being a cheapskate. If you want to go out after sightseeing you will be catching very expensive taxis whenever you want to head back to your hotel and in the long run you will end up spending even more money than if you had stayed somewhere more central. This applies to almost all city vacations. Choose somewhere so in the middle of the places you want to visit you can walk almost everywhere. You can of course rent a car but nowadays parking Downtown in almost every European and American city costs a small fortune.

But It's ON SALE

Going shopping while there is a sale going on is always a good idea but you need to plan beforehand. If you go shopping aimlessly you will return home with products you don't need. This technique can be used for shopping for clothes, groceries, even electronics.

We recommend you start watching the American TV show Hoarders. You will be so horrified by what people keep in the house that you will learn how to be more organized and not to keep crap around. It might seem like a waste of money to start throwing things out and give your house a good clean but you will find you own a lot more stuff than you remembered. No use buying that juicer, you already own one!

Make a list before you head out shopping. Do you really need to buy five t-shirts because they are on sale? Are they really that irresistible? How come you didn't buy them before when you went to that store a month ago? Ask yourself if you really need to fill your life with clutter.

Free Stuff In Your City

Believe it or not there is free entertainment for you to do on your days off. Some cities have special days when museum entrance is free, check their websites and aim

7. Saving Money

towards visiting museums those days. Some culture won't hurt you; we have faith in your cultured status, since you have already bought this book.

Some days there are free movie screenings, or even movie showings in parks. Some cinema websites give out free tickets for movies opening that week.

Going To The Gym

We pretend we don't need exercise but we are not getting any younger and the endorphins will make you feel better if you are fighting depression or just feeling blue. Endorphins are released by exercising, sex, eating spicy food, pain or love.

A gym membership however might weigh down your monthly budget a little bit if you are counting pennies. Most cities have public parks where you can walk and run around and exercise for free or practically nothing. Public swimming pools also cost next to nothing (please wear flip flops at all times, we don't endorse getting athlete's foot).

Another big issue associated with recession, unemployment, money saving and exercising is motivation, so we advise you to use the following tips to keep motivated and fitness ready:

<u>Commit financially</u>. If you sign up for a fitness class the night before, the fact you have paid for it should help you find the motivation to go, so as not to waste the money. Just be careful with this strategy. The goal is to save

money, not do a lot of things, but be even poorer than you were before!

Be productive. Make a list of things you would like to get done every week like 500 sit ups, 10km walking/running, etc. By achieving small goals from your list you will feel more productive and motivated.

Keep to your schedule. We know that lying in and sleeping until late is wonderful but if you schedule appointments that require you to leave the house early you will get more things done. So instead of going to the gym at the end of the day, try going in early. It will give you an energy boost and make you feel more productive as well.

Healthy habits. Keep healthy food in your home/workplace/etc. There is nothing more depressing than spending every day at the gym and seeing no results because you decide that you need an extra-large pizza after every session.

Try other activities. Sometimes you will get the same amount of exercise done by volunteering and leaving the house. You will be rewarded by staying busy, doing good and keeping active.

Use social media to benefit you. Instead of spending all your time stalking other people and feeling miserable, use it to better yourself. Follow websites that inspire you, create a pinterest.com account to save healthy interesting new fitness routines, meal plans and inspirational people. But please do not turn into that annoying person who bought a little gadget or app that posts on your social

7. Saving Money

networking sites that you are going on a run every single damn time. We understand it can be uplifting to have your friends cheer you on whenever you put on a tracksuit and act like a fool, but the other 95% of the people you know are rolling their eyes and thinking some random kind stranger should punch you in the face or steal your stupid phone while you go on your precious jogs.

Starbucks Consumption

Everyone loves a cup of Joe in the morning. On average about 50% of the American population drinks coffee, that's 150 million Americans right there. An espresso costs on average $2.45, so if you drink 20 cups per month (every day in the morning while heading to work) you are spending $50 dollars per month just on coffee. On average a person spends $3.25 at Starbucks every time you go in. That is $65 dollars per month. Your coffee addiction is costing you $780 dollars a year. That is one plane ticket to an awesome transatlantic destination somewhere.

We are not trying to convince you to give up coffee. The three writers of this book would get rather angry if someone took their coffee away from them. But maybe you can cut back or start making some of your coffee at home.

And yes, we know everyone loves the Starbucks Frappuccino. So you can indulge sometimes. We do too.

Personal Loans

Personal loans are a big no no. Loans are necessary tools to buy things like houses, apartments, land and to pay school tuitions. But when you wander into the murky area of getting loans to buy cell phones, vacations and weddings you are doing one of the most stupid things you can do.

Personal loans have extremely high interest rates, so you will end up paying for your new shiny smartphone probably two times its value. Some personal loans have interest rates as high as 10%, maybe even higher. Is that reasonable for you to get married or go on that Greek cruise? No. If you can't afford a vacation out of your own pocket save up so you can afford one next year.

Personal loans should only be used for paying surprise medical bills and bailing someone out of jail. Something unexpected. Save for the rest and pay it out of your pocket.

Carpooling

Do you drive alone to work every morning? How about your colleagues? And you all live near to each other? Maybe you can set up a system where you each take turns driving to work. In the US this is a commonly used system and they even have lanes on freeways especially reserved for carpoolers, so you will actually get to work faster if you are saving gas by sharing a car. In Europe we do drive less and our cars spend less but the amount of money you spend on gas each month might surprise you a little bit.

You can drive to your colleague's house, leave your car there and you both take their car to work, if you don't want that person to have extra trouble all the way to your house or apartment.

7. Saving Money

And hey, you are saving the planet too by not spending as much fuel.

Textbooks

A big expense that most parents have is textbooks for your kids. This is a necessary item that unfortunately might set you back a couple of hundred Euros/Dollars/Pounds every year. Truth is, most books are in perfectly good condition after being read/used. Maybe you have two kids or similar aged cousins and they are lucky enough to be able to exchange books between them.

If you aren't as lucky we propose you look into swapping/buying second hand books from the following options:

<u>Book recycling websites</u>- several new websites provide this service such as textbookrecycling.com. These websites even donate a percentage of what they offer you to one of the charitable organizations they support.

<u>Rent a book options</u> - websites such as bookrenter.com offer book renting with free shipping and free returns. What's not to love?

<u>Book donations</u> - there are several places in each country that accept used books that you can go donate or apply to receive. Some are even for college graduates such as collegebudget.com that focuses on saving students money on text books and helping students with their loans.

Book swapping - text4swap.com is a great site to help students in the US save money and go green by swapping books. All you need to do is enter the name of the book you are looking for and find who has it. Find the site for your country and take advantage.

Bank Accounts

Sometimes you need to spend money to save money. There are a few examples of this spread throughout this book. Many people, for example, would think that paying for a bank account is crazy, and will just go for the free option. While this seems sensible on the surface, a paid account could end up saving you more than you think.

As an example we'll look at the cost and benefits of Gary's bank account. Gary has a Royalties Gold Account with the Royal Bank of Scotland. He pays £12.95 per month. But the benefits received far outweigh the cost.

First up is mobile phone insurance. You get free cover for a phone up to £1000 in value. Since no phones cost that much, any phone in existence is covered, as is up to £1500 in calls made on it before you reported it stolen. The cheapest comparable insurance we were able to find online weighed in at £6.99 a month. Though, having said that, the website did not fill us with confidence.

You also get travel insurance. 5 Star Defaqto rating. A similar policy online is likely to cost at least £160. If you work out the monthly cost, it is more than the monthly cost of the account.

7. Saving Money

You also get free car breakdown cover from Green Flag. To get the same cover buying direct from Green Flag would cost at least £45.

Paying for that bank account doesn't seem so silly now does it?

Here are some more benefits you get for your £12.95

- 10% off Flights
- Free UK airport lounge access on international flights
- Discounts of up to 60% on hotel bookings
- 2 year extended warranty for everything bought with your debit card
- 25% off at 700 UK restaurants
- 25% off concert tickets
- 10% of home insurance

Check your banking websites, see what they will give you and how much it will cost. Paying for the account may mean you can save money elsewhere. If the net total is a gain for you, then it's worth paying the bank!

Saving Money Is Not Always Worth It.

Always be cautious when saving money. Sometimes things are cheap for a reason. For example, Parcel2Go are a web based courier booking service. They are normally cheaper than anyone else, but the service obtained, as well as their

Troikapocalypse

customer service when contacting them to complain, can only be described as completely woeful. Don't just assume cheaper is better!

We hope these tips help you to take a good look at your expenses and start saving more than you have so far. There are always corners you can cut without making yourself feel more miserable.

8. Yay! You're a Geek!

We know we shouldn't stereotype, but we want to have some fun with this so forgive us. Chances are if you are a geek, you are pretty un-phased by the economic slowdown that is happening around the world. Why?

Geek Jobs

CareerCast launched its annual list of top jobs to have in 2012 and you don't have to be a genius to find a pattern if you compare it to lists made in the past twenty years.

It pays off to be a geek. Apparently more than being a doctor, a humanitarian or an architect. Those years you spent playing video games which allowed you to get a job as a computer programmer may have saved you from certain Doom at the hands of today's harsh economic climate.

Jobs directly related to computers on the CareerCast list occupy spots number 1, 8, 9 and 15. This list takes into account the availability of job prospects, salary, work conditions and your future employability if you wish to relocate and change companies. We aren't even counting jobs like Mathematician and Actuary, which are high up on the list and are, let's be frank, extremely geeky jobs that rely on MATH (the horror).

8. Yay! You're a Geek!

While your classmates in high school were perfecting the art of beer pong you were home playing Quake and Diablo. And that probably saved your career. Your parents, instead of framing your diploma, should be bronzing your PlayStation or your keyboard.

We are just looking at the wonderful world of geekiness in terms of salaries. But what about costs? You might argue geeks spend a lot of money on video games, going to conventions, books, DVD's, etc. But they are smart buyers and they use the internet to their advantage. They look and know where the best deals are for plane tickets, hotel discounts, sales on websites like Amazon and other similar sites. You might think someone is spending a lot of money in San Diego to hang out with their peers and hope to get all those autographs they've been pining over and buy a ton of action figures, but let's face it: they are smart buyers.

Geeks will also try to come up with other ways to entertain themselves outside of work creatively. They will build websites, create other means of income. Who knows, even write a book. Why yes, this book is a perfect example of three geeks trying to use their talents to get some leverage. Try to use your geek talents for good instead of evil. Maybe you have a smart business idea buzzing around in your head that you always wanted to try but were too afraid to get it off the paper. We should reference the chapter "Is Crime the answer" here before you start planning to take over the world with your army of zombies and sharks with lasers attached to their heads. But maybe you can create an app, or start a web design business, or save baby pandas with a new environmentalist website. You just need to turn off Skyrim or at least start using your time while you're not working in a more creative way.

Famous Geeks

Here are a few examples of geeks who used their talent to create highly profitable companies who mostly do good instead of evil (although in Zuckerberg's case that is debatable).

We of course have to mention **Steve Jobs**, the genius behind Apple. iPhones, iPads, iMacs... the list goes on. Jobs grabbed a dying company who was surpassed by the PC and reimagined it, creating products people crave for due to their simplicity and design. Apple products have followers, not consumers, it is a religion.

Mark Zuckerberg created Facebook. Do you have a Facebook account? Of course you do, everyone does, how else could you check up on your exes and feel unpopular or way too popular? He went to Harvard and developed Facebook from a silly program he was building in his free time where college students could rate their fellow classmates. He is now one of the 100 richest men in the world.

Evan Williams and **Biz Stone** created Twitter. Twitter of course is more of a fad and we keep waiting for it to die out but the truth is that celebrities love showing you what they had for lunch and how fabulous their lives are compared to yours. Twitter allows them to do that as long as they ignore the scary stalkerish fans hanging out there.

8. Yay! You're a Geek!

We need to mention Google, of course. **Larry Page**, one of its co-founders, has a net worth that makes **Bill Gates** squirm a little bit (not too much, he still owns Microsoft which means he still practically owns the world). Whenever you Google something, you are buying Mr. Page and his associates a new yacht.

The point is, use your powers of geekdom for good. Write that book, start that video game idea, plan that movie out. Don't just complain about how the world is taking a bad turn and how the ice caps are melting and the Amazon jungle is dying. They are, but we get to do something about it. If it makes us a little extra pocket money, awesome. If it doesn't, well at least you tried, and hopefully had some fun doing it.

9. How the Sun Killed Our Economy

A Melting Pot Of... Just Melting

During the summer of 2012, there were days when the temperature reached almost 40°C in Lisbon (or 104°F for you Americans). While we pondered why the Sun decided to punish us, we came to a brilliant conclusion: we can blame our economy on the weather.

We wanted to say the Sun killed our economy and that would be an amazing name for a chapter (so we are still using it) but the truth is that Iceland's economy tanked first and a heat wave in Iceland is when it takes 10 seconds instead of 5 for your face to freeze after you go outside. So our conclusion is that extreme weather conditions influence the economy. How you ask? Do you really think anybody wants to do hard labour when it is so hot outside even your dog refuses to go out and prefers to hold it in instead of having his own paws glued to the melting pavement? No. And your dog is smarter than you are apparently.

Portugal, Spain and Greece all suffer from extreme heat during the summer. People that can't take days off in those hot July and August months have to drag themselves to work while others go to the beach and drink cool beer and don't think about the office.

9. How the Sun Killed Our Economy

The reverse situation is also true. Cold weather is great for practicing winter sports. But when it's so cold that you can't feel your own face, and you look like a Michelin dummy with all those layers, you don't really want to do anything serious like actual work. The cold is perfect for skiing, snowboarding and having snowball fights. Remember that cold means icy roads and sidewalks. Have you tried walking to work when everything is frozen and it takes you 45 minutes to get to the supermarket that is 5-minutes away? It is not amusing.

In this new theory we are not taking into account countries such as Finland, Sweden and the United Arab Emirates. There are always exceptions to the rule and they are freaks of nature. Or maybe they just have very good indoor climate control methods. Electricity is expensive, and if poorer countries abused air conditioning privileges, like the United States does, we would not be able to afford luxuries like "food", "health insurance" or "clean water". So people endure the warm weather. You just learn how to work more slowly.

We think the solution here is to divide Europe in terms of labour. We will now use Mediterranean countries for Tourism only. You want a great beach, go there. Germany and the like can house big factories and do the hard labour. The United Kingdom can house services since it rains all the time and people need to stay indoors to avoid catching a cold. France and the Netherlands can concentrate on agriculture and cheese (they love their cows). French wine! Who doesn't love delicious wine? French cheese, wine and tulips everywhere, it's the perfect Europe.

A unified Europe means a Europe with more ice drinks, cheese, wine and walks on the beach. Pass the sunblock please.

Penis!

Another alternative theory we want to explore associates penises with economic development. A recent study published by the University of Helsinki titled *"Male Organ and Economic Growth: Does Size Matter"* (yes, seriously, we are not making this up) took a wilder approach than we did and tried to establish a correlation between penis size and economic growth, using data compiled from 1960 to 1985. It compares the gross domestic product (GDP) of different countries around the world and the length of male penises. This study concludes that large penises lead to a lower GDP, This study does not include oil-producing countries (nobody needs a big penis when they're driving a Lamborghini apparently).

Countries like South Korea, Japan and Singapore have high GDP values and very small penis length statistics. Other countries like Sudan, Ghana and Congo excel in penis sizes but have an extremely low evolution in the GDP. We know this study will worry a lot of men from developed countries, but hey guys, at least you can pay your bills right?

Read the study, you will find it very entertaining. Testosterone and self-esteem apparently might be more influential to the world economy than academic studies and education. This paper might be a little destructive for

9. How the Sun Killed Our Economy

the male ego though, and slightly unfair. If we claim to live in an equal opportunity society where women play an equally important part in the world economy as men, maybe there should be a study made on amount of orgasms versus economic growth, or breast size, or something equally as arbitrary.

We prefer our theory; weather is so much more subjective. We wanted to present a real study on this but after some research the closest we found was an article called "*US Economic Sensibility to Weather Variability*". It shows how changes in temperature affects tourism, how severe weather conditions affect crops, transportation, damage to business and real estate, etc. It is not exactly what we were looking for, but it gives a new insight on how hot weather might create more adverse conditions for a stable economy. It is not just a question of being lazy. Heat waves bring fires and destruction to crops and forests, and occasionally can spread to residential and industrial areas, resulting in damage often running into the millions.

The Scorching Heat And The Four Horsemen

2013 will be a year of many changes according to many newspapers and magazines. Bad things are coming. And apparently the news outlets are still on an Apocalypse kick because many of them are still using End of Times analogies. Recently there have been talks of War or Famine coming. Sadly no super smart writers have tried to associate the Conquest Horseman with anything, because frankly it is hard to be witty about a word like "Conquest". Famine and War sound so much more ominous. And

Troikapocalypse

Death, Death is impossible to beat in terms of newspaper sales.

Several droughts have ruined crops worldwide. In a year corn prices have gone up 25% and soybean prices 17%. While this does not seem like much for a person in a developed country, in developing countries these increases in prices are severe and can lead to widespread hunger in countries where these basic items make up much of a person's diet. Americans spend about 10% of their salary on food, including eating in restaurants. A citizen in Kenya or Pakistan spends around 45% of their income on food. Restaurants are completely beyond most of them.

Scorching temperatures and lack of rain has seen crops wither and die, along with hurricanes, floods and wildfires. Mother Nature has shown us the fragility of our food production chain.

In America, crops have been affected by the worst drought in fifty years. When conditions outstrip America's ability to cope, even with all their technological advancement, you can imagine how third world countries will be affected

A recent study undertaken by Oxfam (Oxford Committee for Famine Relief) says that food prices could double by 2030. According to this confederation of organizations we are headed to a permanent food crisis which will require a radical shake up of the entire global food industry.

Oxfam research forecasts international prices of some food items, such as cereal, could rise by as much as 180% by 2030, with half of that rise due to the impact of climate

9. How the Sun Killed Our Economy

change. The World Bank warned last month that rising food prices have pushed 44 million people into poverty since 2010.

Prepare to start enjoying the taste of bugs. That's right. There are already several international studies looking into how to introduce insects as an accepted food source in western nations. Other countries are much more open to this concept. It's nothing too new though. You might not know this but red beetles are used by a few very well-known international brands as red food colouring. We won't get into all the uses of insects in this way, as we suspect we'd put you off most of the things you like to eat. Another unusual food source could also help. Algae. While not terribly appealing, algae is high in protein, fibre and various vitamins, while being low in fat. Much like insects, convincing people it's not disgusting will most likely be the biggest obstacle to its adoption.

We live in a baffling world where it's cheaper to eat at a fast food chain than to buy vegetables in a supermarket. It's a little silly that this problem is not considered to be a major issue by governments everywhere.

If you are a foodie (sometimes spelled foody), an informal term for people who love food and enjoy experimenting with it, you might be in for some rough times. Unless you actually like bugs. In that case you are all set and have no need to worry.

War

Troikapocalypse

If Famine doesn't cause chaos in 2013, could War? It's not as directly connected to temperatures so it might not belong in this chapter, but since we're using the horsemen analogy we will continue.

Conspiracy theorists are predicting a war between Iran and Israel. We know this is not a new prediction, and these two countries are not exactly the best of friends but it is still a scary scenario considering the likelihood of others becoming involved.

Since July 2012, several international sanctions have been imposed on Iran in an attempt to curtail its nuclear program, which may, or may not, include the development of nuclear weapons. While it sounds like a noble idea, this has severely damaged the country's economy and Iran has accused the West of an "all-out war". Considering that 80% of Iran's income comes from oil exports, you can imagine the toll this has taken. The sanctions have devalued the Iranian rial to record lows against the Dollar. This has led to the Iranian people finding it increasingly difficult to buy basic food items. No money means being unable to buy even the most basic, and necessary items.

Iran has said it has no problems with America. It has stated several times it does, however, hate Israel. These two countries have a long history of not being best buddies. What would happen if Israel and Iran actually went to war again?

Some pessimists predict this could be World War 3. But why is this related to Europe? Well, if you can fathom the

9. How the Sun Killed Our Economy

meaning of a World War, it could involve everyone. What with wars often not remaining limited to the original combatants. If this happens, you can stop worrying about your bank loans and start worrying about that big mushroom on the horizon that looks eerily like pictures you've seen in History books of Hiroshima and Nagasaki.

Maybe the Mediterranean way of enjoying the sun is not such a bad attitude after all. Maybe those of us working from sunrise to sunset will be really upset when we're either starving or dying and realize that we could have drunk a lot more beer with our feet curled in the sand. There is no use worrying about mundane problems when the world you know could come to an end at any moment.

10. Pack Your Bags, Let's Emigrate!

Expectation Versus Reality

So it turns out you are over qualified for all the available jobs. You are young, eager and keep getting job offers for crap internships, where employers treat you as though they are doing you a favour for by putting you to work, from dusk till dawn, in exchange for pocket change.

Unfortunately, that is Europe nowadays. Statistics show that almost 50% of recent graduates cannot find a job. Any job. In some countries, since you have never had a job, you are not included in the unemployment statistics, and can't claim unemployment benefits.

So what is the solution? Stick around and try to find something? Be an entrepreneur and start your own business? Or just pack up and leave?

Well, if you are in Greece, Portugal or Spain you probably should have already left. We know leaving family and friends behind is not easy but you are not the captain of that ship, and as such are not expected to go down with it, but you do need to realize you need some sort of plan or a job already set up. Dreams and reality are often very different things. Quite a lot of dreamers end up working in telemarketing or the customer service industry in countries

10. Pack Your Bags, Let's Emigrate!

like the United Kingdom or Germany. This is not a bad job per se, but it was probably not what those people envisioned when they moved. Nobody is waiting for you at Heathrow Airport with the keys to your new Aston Martin.

You need to balance expectations against your dreams of grandeur. You also need to realize you are still that immigrant escaping a bad situation, looking for something better. You are, in most cases, not doing your new country a huge favour by showing up. You might have done your old country a favour by leaving though; you won't count for the ugly statistics that say your home sucks.

So you decided to become an emigrant. Now what? There are a couple of factors that will either make or break your emigration experience. Some might sound obvious, others might surprise you.

Regardless of where you end up, please put in the effort. Learn the language and mingle with the locals. Don't isolate yourself in a community of immigrants. You should try to integrate into the local community. This is your new home, don't hold onto the past.

If you do become one of those annoying immigrants who keep reminding everyone that their home country was better, just move back. We know it sounds harsh but if your new adventure is a source of anxiety and not an exciting opportunity there is no use trying to make it work for years on end.

If your dream is to work in a call centre, make it fun. Move to India. You can wear a bindi and eat curry and you will get to speak with people all over the world. You will even pretend your name is something Anglo Saxon, like John or Mary.

In Portugal even the government suggested young people shouldn't stick around. Which is a shame. Your own country thinks you are delirious for having studied and not wanting to work at a fast food chain flipping burgers.

If you do stick around, become a politician. But never do it in Iceland, ever. They actually have to take responsibility for their actions. It's so horrifying, you steal and you go to jail. What next? Politicians paying their own taxes and driving economic cars? Giving money to charity? Iceland is totally not the example to follow with their social justice, people paying for their crimes and going to jail. The fact their economy is bouncing back also sounds very strange and unusual. Not at all the normal European way of doing things.

Just do it the Portuguese way. Sink a country further into debt and move to Paris afterwards to get a philosophy degree in a fancy university like the Sorbonne. Now that's quality emigration right there.

This all brings us to another issue. You should move to a country where you think you will fit in. Do you hate spicy food? Unless you want to starve to death, India and Thailand are not your best choices. Don't like the cold? Why did you take that job in Norway then?

If we look at the statistics presented by the INE (National Statistics Institute of Portugal) we can see that between 2009 and 2011 Portuguese emigration rose significantly

10. Pack Your Bags, Let's Emigrate!

mainly amongst 20 to 30 year olds. If we analyse the annual emigration by sex, although it is maintaining a similar pattern of emigration percentage between the number of men and women leaving Portugal (13.589 men versus 10.171 women in 2010 and 9.665 versus 7.234 in 2009), it is still a bit scary that men usually are the first ones out the country. The 2012 ratio between men and women in the country is 107 women per every 100 men. Wait.. So why are all the men leaving?

CNN published an article in August 15th 2012 called "Portuguese head to Mozambique to escape Eurozone crisis" where it presents examples where Portuguese youngsters decide to go back to the old colonies to be at the forefront of opportunities in Africa. Why Africa you ask?

We think that statistically a few years from now the country will be ruled by a bunch of older aged lesbians. It can only mean that heterosexual couples and single men are moving to Africa to escape the Lesbians. That or Africa's gross domestic product is growing by an average 7%. Who knows?

Either way, we believe you might need some pointers on how to emigrate so you can jump on the bandwagon.

Starting off

You might want to save up a little money before you decide to embark on your little adventure abroad. First you need money to rent an apartment or a room and some of these ask for a deposit (some ask for a very high deposit of at least 2 months' rent up front). You also need to count with at least one to two months of job hunting before you actually find something (if you left without a job already lined up). If you leave your country with just the clothes on your back you might end up living in your car (if you drove there) or accepting some desperate low-paying job just to be able to eat. And for low-paying jobs you probably could have just stayed where you were and not gone abroad. Why move to a whole different country just to work in a coffee shop, struggling with the language and the bills?

Some websites allow you to search for a job abroad before you leave, allowing you to have job interviews lined up before you get there. This is an extremely good idea. Make sure you trust those job websites and that those job opportunities really exist. We have heard stories of people going abroad and ending up working in tomato fields in Spain after being promised a job that didn't really exist. Others know you are desperate for a job and will throw sand in your eyes and try to scam you. Don't be naive and research everything. Should you pay thousands of euros for a job opportunity? No, they are supposed to be paying you! If it looks like a scam, it is a scam.

Visas

Visas are also another issue we need to address. While it is wonderful to dream big and move to a whole new country, it might be easier to move within Europe and take advantage of the "mobility of people" part of the Schengen Agreement. Starting your new life by being an illegal immigrant should be used by war refugees and not by graduate students trying to make it. We would all love to move to a rich country and make five times what we do

10. Pack Your Bags, Let's Emigrate!

right now but we do believe you should do it the legal way, and not the "let's hope I don't get deported" way.

Last, but not least, for you to be a proper emigrant, you need to send money home, so you better have left behind some family members or people really close to you that are not doing very well financially. It's tradition, after all. We are kidding of course, but a lot of emigrants still send money back home and invest in real estate in their home countries. Since we are staying behind and enduring the crisis while you are off in some amazing country with a great life, we support your investments in real estate and your help in recovering the country you so cowardly abandoned.

If you are going to leave us behind, keep sending those checks!

The strange (but not necessarily bad) part of leaving

The act of leaving your home country fundamentally changes you. You will learn and adapt to the new environment that you live in. You may find you acquire new mannerisms and opinions, coloured by the people you surround yourself with.

When you move abroad, like a child, you will have to re-learn a lot of things that you took for granted. Grocery shopping for example. When you are in a place where you do not know a lot of people your day to day life will also change. You will probably have to spend a lot of time on your own, maybe eating by yourself with only a book or your mobile phone to keep you company. Although difficult, this experience can enrich you. You will start to appreciate the quiet moments and little things you never noticed before. You will find solace in new activities and places and a new kind of love for the people you left behind. Hopefully you will also begin to build a new circle of friends to ease the transition.

A common thing experienced by those who move abroad is fear. It is something that slowly fades, but can remain in one form or another for a long time. In the beginning you will be afraid you won't make any friends. Maybe that you won't fit in at work. You may fear not being able to learn the language or to adapt to the city you are living in. But as time goes by, as you settle in, that fear will change and you will start to be anxious about what you left behind. As time passes people move on, get married, create families, children grow up and, unfortunately, people pass away. Most importantly, people change. You will understand how difficult it is to answer the "are you ever going back home?" question.

When you are back "home" (although home is where the heart is, you will probably always think of home as the country where you grew up), conversations appear out of context, people will be worried about things that you either no longer care for, or understand. Your experiences will be fundamentally different.

You will also find out who your real friends are, because when people are away it is easy to forget them. You will find people that instead of being happy for you, are envious of your new found courage to go in search of a happier life. You will find people that are so heartbroken

10. Pack Your Bags, Let's Emigrate!

and hurt that you left that they can no longer be your friends. Hopefully you will understand, or at least forgive them.

Another issue usually no one ever mentions is that when you live abroad, you will need to work hard. Not only do you have to manage your new found life, but you will have to make time to plan for your old one. Catching up with friends and family and planning visits and holidays to go and see them will become part of the norm.

Not everything is negative, as Catherine Transler states in her e-book for *"Dealing with loneliness when living abroad, scientific insights and practical tips for expats and internationals"*. You might learn how to be more open and tolerant individual. You will find yourself starting conversations with people you would probably be too shy to talk to before.

Art Markman, Ph.D. contends that living abroad can make you more creative. We agree with this theory and add that you will become more independent. Not having the usual network of people to help you will force you to leave your comfort zone and experience new things.

In conclusion, when you buy a one-way ticket, get on that plane and call another place home, this comes with a price. Your heart cannot be in two places at once if you want to make it work. You will always wonder what you might be missing and if you made the right decision.

However, when things are rough due to external factors like the current economic situation, you may not have a choice. Regardless, just try to enjoy the ride, wherever it may take you.

Troikapocalypse

11. Is Crime The Answer?

We are well aware bills keep piling up. And let's face it, it is all a question of math. If your salary is X and your expenses are Y (fixed expenses) and Z (variable expenses like doctor's appointments, a few dinners out at restaurants, shopping, car trouble, etc.), sometimes X does not mark the spot. And you start digging into your savings just to keep your life from going into a downward spiral.

If you have ever seen the television show Breaking Bad this is a good example of a good man crossing quite a few lines to save his family. In the show the main character discovers he has cancer and the only way he can figure he can pay for the treatments and make sure his family is provided for in case he dies is to start making meth in a drug laboratory. Being a chemistry teacher, he is fairly good at the actual drug making, but everything else that comes with being a drug dealer are beyond his ability to deal with.

His life spirals out of control quickly but it's very interesting to think how much it takes for an individual to cross that fine moral line. It's that age-old question: if your child was dying would you steal some medicine to save his life? Most people would

11. Is Crime The Answer?

probably do it, which is what makes us human. We make sacrifices and put ourselves in danger to protect our loved ones. Not all that long ago, any kind of theft would have seen you put to death. A far cry from today where cheating a little on your taxes can make a huge difference in the long run for some. Maybe we were too hard on the Greeks for their evading ways?

We do not think you should turn to crime as a possible way out. There are always better solutions. Looking for a higher paid job, even getting a second job, should always come first. And we know you are tired of working and feeling like you achieved nothing. Most people believe that a fast food chain is "beneath" them, but believe us, being embarrassed by flipping burgers might be less traumatizing than trading cigarette cartons for sexual favours in some prison in the middle of nowhere.

We know the government steals too. We all see the news and we know that there is no worst scourge of the earth than the one of the "politician". Frankly someone has to make the tough economic decisions in the world but we should follow Iceland's example and throw the corrupt politicians in jail. Somehow, Democracy has failed us and these people still get away with stealing and cheating and embezzling. You just need to remember an important rule: you will get caught and the rules of immunity do not apply to you.

Desperation leads a person to do crazy things but crime is the riskiest of all professions.

Bank robberies and petty crime have been increasing all over Europe. We do not need to be experts on the economy to see this. Citizens cannot pay their bills. Unemployment has risen. Crime and desperation are often directly related to each other. We are seeing a rise in carjacking's, bank robberies, domestic violence, illegal weapons being sold on the black market, and, unfortunately, deaths due to these crimes.

Starting A Revolution

Some people are filled with anger. Over pay cuts, social injustice, even the bank that keeps stealing their money. Others just want to cause trouble. When there's a crisis it usually comes hand in hand with social unrest. And while most people at a demonstration behave and really are showing their discontent by marching down big avenues holding signs, while not being violent, there are always idiots out there who use this opportunity to vent their anger by provoking the police, creating the impression the entire protest was based on violence.

Violence is never the answer. If you decide to protest, do it peacefully and don't cause trouble for the people around you. You want to torch stores and businesses? Other people who are probably as badly off as you own

11. Is Crime The Answer?

those. If we were the owners of the shop you just threw a Molotov cocktail at, we would not feel the need to sympathise with your cause.

Demonstrations are fine if you live in a country that allows them, but hurting others is not. Yes, we know this part isn't extremely funny but it had to be said. So before you decide your way to show your anger is to be a street criminal, try to get a job.

Domestic violence also increases in times of strife, as does homicide. Surprisingly most homicide cases are acts of passion, so usually they are within a household. Husband shoots wife, wife stabs husband. Most people cannot avoid bringing their work problems home and they take them out on family members. Domestic violence is nothing to be laughed at and if this is your case, get out while you can, it generally never gets better.

Leave The Real Stuff For The Professionals

You are not the kingpin of crime so you may have to take a new approach and maybe improve the locks in your apartment or not walk around dark streets before you start thinking about joining the Evil League of Evil. If you are reading this you are probably a possible victim and not a future entrepreneur of criminal activities in your neighbourhood.

How about white-collar crime? Don't even think about going there. That's a very tight-knit group, they are almost like a secret society, and not everyone is allowed in. They have had years and years of practice and newcomers are generally not welcomed with open arms. After all, they're the ones taking your money, lowering your salaries and making you want to turn to a life of crime.

The Soap Method

Desperate times call for desperate measures. We suggest you start doing the following. Whenever you think you can get away with a crime really consider if it's worth going to jail for. You probably have never been to jail (statistically, we could be wrong). A jail is not a playground. Can you handle the thought of being incarcerated twenty four hours a day for several months or years just because you thought you could get away with it? Yeah, we didn't think so.

Next time that work bank account calls out to you because it looks oh so easy to embezzle from, think of your good friend Bubba (or Carlota, we believe in equal opportunity and women can be as mischievous as men) waiting for you to take that shower with you and just waiting for you to drop that bar of soap.

12. Entertainment

No one likes to be bored. We all do things we find fun. The problem is that the majority of the things we do cost money, and these costs are not always obvious at the time. Those times you look at your bank balance and wonder where your money went? It is all the little things that seem like nothing at the time that are to blame.

Now we're not going to suggest that you shouldn't do these things. But there are always areas where you can save some cash simply by recognising what you are spending.

Some of it is pretty simple. Do you buy a coffee on the way to work? Do you and some friends go to a coffee shop for a cup or 3 while you sit and chat? Well the quick solution here would be don't. Coffee is expensive. Incredibly so when you count it up, making it yourself is way cheaper. Buying a lavish coffee machine may seem like an extravagance, but if you are no longer buying all those coffees, it will pay for itself a lot sooner than you think. Of course that increases the hassle involved, sometimes you just want a coffee, without all the hassle of actually making it. Is the coffee shop further down the road cheaper? It is? Have you tried the coffee? Unless you think the more expensive stuff is vastly better coffee and you really don't want to drink the other stuff, save yourself the cash. If your £3.50 coffee just became £2.50, and you buy 5 a week,

12. Entertainment

that's potentially £260 extra per year in your pocket. That's around €330 or $410.

The chances are you are buying more than 5 a week though!

The Idiot Box

Another area where many people haemorrhage money is watching TV. How much are you paying for satellite or cable TV? Do you have more accessible TV channels than there are days in the year? There's no doubt some cash to be saved here.

Another option would be to just get rid of it. The amount of TV that can be watched online is rising all the time. While the legality of some of these options is questionable, no one has ever been prosecuted for watching TV online. The most you would need to contend with would be the website itself being shut down, necessitating the finding of another one.

There are also an increasing number of free, legal, options for watching online, as well as some options that charge. The latter normally being far cheaper than the cable or satellite package you aim to replace.

Now a lot of these online options are locked to particular countries. Fortunately that's easily solved.

This will cost you, but we think the benefits are worth it. You need the VPN UK & USA package from www.streamvia.com

Depending on what currency you prefer, this will cost $4.99/€5.99/$7.99 per month. I know we are trying to save cash here, but stay with us, there are good reasons to pay it. With their SmartStream DNS servers you enter a couple of IP addresses into your PC/Mac/Phone/Tablet/Games console and the services below work just fine.

UK Services

- BBC iPlayer
- 4OD (channel 4 on demand)
- ITV Player
- Demand 5 (channel 5 on demand)
- Sky Go
- Netflix UK
- Spotify

American Services

- Amazon instant video
- Hulu
- Fox
- PBS
- NBC
- ABC Go
- Netflix USA
- Pandora

This is not a complete list by any means. Pretty much anything that normally requires you to be in the UK or America, works. A few of them, like Netflix, will want you

12. Entertainment

to part with cash; in this case all you need is a card to pay with. They let you sign up using a Facebook account nowadays; you won't even need an address, beyond the billing address. Depending on which site you sign up on, Netflix costs £5.99 or $7.99 per month. We'd recommend signing up on the American site, it's cheaper!

We should point out that this is not illegal, though it is likely to violate the Netflix terms of use, meaning they could cancel your account. To be fair, their terms of use say *"We reserve the right to terminate or restrict your use of our service, without notice, for any or no reason whatsoever"*. Though in reality, as long as you give them cash, they are unlikely to care.

Gaming

Spent the last 8 hours watching TV? Don't want to do it anymore, but have no desire to do something else? Well, how about some games?

Let's look at the options. Assuming you're not the kind of lunatic who bought one of those little handheld things, and you are not woefully out of date, you have 3 options. We can discount the Wii, unless you are an old lady, in which case be careful, you could break a hip! So we have two options.

If you want to play games, and spend less money doing it, the Xbox is not the machine you want. Xbox Live costs if you want it to be useful.

A PS3 is a far better investment nowadays. First, unlike

Xbox Live, you can play games online for free. Second, it has a built in Blu-ray player. While you might not have been too bothered about getting a Blu-ray player, if you can incidentally lay your hands on one, why not?

The real reason the PS3 should be the machine of choice for anyone wanting to play games on a budget, is the PlayStation Plus service. Yes, this will cost you, but stay with us while we explain why you should pay for it.

PlayStation Plus has been around for a few years now, but until recently it wasn't exactly great. Someone at Sony though seems to have grown some sense, as recently they launched a new feature of the service that they call "Instant Game Collection".

While Microsoft will charge you just to be able to play games online against other people, that has always been free on the PS3. That hasn't changed. Plus is a subscription service which comes in two flavours. 3 months, or 1 year. A 3 month subscription costing, depending on your location, £11.99 / €14.99 / $17.99. The full year is £39.99 / €49.99 / $49.99. The full year works at around the average price of 1 new game.

Almost everyone with a games console buys at least a few games per year. Some buy them used to save some money, but even then, the total cost quickly mounts up. With the instant games collection, you are immediately allowed to download, for free, 10 games. It's not always the same 10 games, some are removed and new ones added, but the genius lies in that while you remain a subscriber, even after a game is removed from the list, as long as you added

12. Entertainment

it to your download list, it is yours to keep for as long as you keep subscribing. With Sony promising that you will get 48+ games per year, paying roughly the same price to Microsoft just so you can play games online suddenly seems rather crazy.

The one caveat here is that if you stop subscribing, you will not be able to play these games any more. Though should you reactivate your subscription at any time, the games will be there waiting for you. Any that were available and gone while you were not subscribed, you will miss out on being able to download.

For the cost, it really is great value. Not all the games are full price titles. But the free stuff you get over a year is estimated at around $1200.

At the time of writing, the games available to download in the EU store (there are slight differences between regions) are –

- Lara Croft & the Guardian of Light
- Saints Row 2
- Deus Ex: Human Revolution
- Darksiders
- Renegade Ops
- Outland
- Oddworld: Strangers' Wrath HD
- inFamous 2
- Motorstorm Apocalypse
- LittleBigPlanet 2

Troikapocalypse

Three of these are scheduled to be removed and replaced with new games in the next 3 weeks.

One other thing you may want to consider if signing up for Playstation Plus is that it might be a good idea to buy a bigger hard drive for your PS3 to store all the games on!

If you want to get your gaming fix, yet not pay anything for it, there are some options for that too. DC Universe is an online game available on both the PC and the PS3, that is totally free to download and play. There are additional add-ons you can buy, a subscription package available giving extra benefits, but it isn't a pay to win situation. The content you can pay for does not give any in game advantage over not paying.

Moving away from the consoles, there are loads of these "Free 2 Play" games. Some of the more recognised ones being, The Lord of the Rings Online, Everquest 2, Microsoft Flight, Star Trek Online... The list goes on. Free 2 play is the big thing in gaming now, as companies are learning that people tend to buy the little extras. Player numbers and revenue generated almost always rise when a game goes free to play.

The upside for you? No need to buy anything, and no subscription fees. Your level of investment in the game, both in terms of time and money, is as much or as little as you like.

If you are a Mac owner, looking to kill some time before the mothership comes to collect you, the pickings are a bit

12. Entertainment

slimmer. If the mission issued to you by high command back on the homeworld means you categorically must own a Mac, then Steam would be your best bet for cheap games.

Steam, which is available to download from their site at - http://store.steampowered.com/ is a digital distribution platform for games. It's most often used by PC users, but it has a growing collection of games for macs. While the prices of games is normally not much cheaper than any other method of buying them, they always have a selection of games on special offer, and every few months they have a massive sale, with discounts of 75% or more being common.

Should a Mac owner one day defect, becoming a proud member of the PC owning master race, the feature they refer to as "Steamplay" would mean that all those games you bought on the mac will be available to you on the PC as well. Your initial purchase was just not the Mac version, but the PC version as well.

The reverse also holds true. Should any of you decide to replace your magnificent PC with an overpriced Mac, if you have previously bought games that are also available on the Mac, that version would be also be available to you.

If leaving the house and spending time with others is more your thing, then a few minor adjustments to your normal routine could result in the contents of your bank account remaining where they are a little longer.

Feed Me!

Troikapocalypse

A major cause of unexpectedly empty bank account syndrome, is eating out. Even though people often decide to go somewhere cheap, the result is often that people delude themselves into thinking they are saving money when they really aren't. A justification like *"It's cheap in here, so I can afford to order that crazy huge steak I'll never finish"* might make you feel better about it, but all you are doing is wasting a lot of meat and not saving any money.

Instead of going for lunch to that nice little restaurant you and your friends like, why not try that little cafe nearby that charges less than half the price? The food might not be great, but a lot of these places can surprise. Your potatoes might not come in odd shapes, your vegetables not cut at odd angles, but they will be a lot cheaper, and quite possibly there will be more of them. Restaurants having perfected the art of selling small portions for high prices.

Now we're not saying you should do this all the time, but try some cheaper places, you may find some great places where the quality is far better than you'd expect from the price. Keep the fancier places for special occasions.

As well as taking into account the location of your meal, there are numerous online methods of bringing the cost down. Groupon often has large discounts available for restaurants. Discounts of 50% or more are fairly common. If you are lucky enough to have a few of these deals in your local area in a short space of time you should grab them. Not only do you get a great deal on a night out, but some of

12. Entertainment

your friends do too. How many of them depends on the specifics of the deal.

Groupon operate pretty much everywhere and they offer deals on far more than just restaurants. It's the type of site you should visit once a day, every day. Most of what they are offering probably won't be stuff you would go for, but you don't want to miss the day they do have something you want. Discounts of the size they offer are not to be ignored. It's also a fantastic way to stock up on birthday and Christmas presents.

Another way to save on eating out is to join a diners' club. Two of the biggest diners clubs in the UK are Tastecard & Hi-Life Diners club. Your membership in these clubs entitles you to 50% off your bill.

These memberships do cost, so you might want to get a spreadsheet made up to see if they would benefit you. Hi-Life provides you with access to over 4,000 restaurants in the UK & Ireland and costs £69.99 for a year, or £84.99 for a year of the platinum membership. Platinum getting you better weekend availability, a secondary standard card to give to someone and some exclusive restaurants with some top chefs, for example - Michael Caines, Marco Pierre White & Gary Rhodes.

Tastecard provides access to, at the time of writing, 6,534 restaurants in the UK & Ireland. The normal price is £79.95 a year, but new members can often get it for £59.95 per year, and if that slight discount is not enough to get you to commit right off, they also offer a free 1 month trial card so you can test it out for yourself. Even if you don't plan to buy the year's membership, you would be foolish not to take them up on the free month offer.

Still on the subject of food, if you are a regular passenger on UK trains, then a Bitecard will get you 20% any orders at a selection of food and drink vendors in train stations. The best part about this card is that it is entirely free. You just register on the site and they send you one.

Look for similar things wherever you are. Ask your friends if they have heard of anything like this. You may be surprised at some of the opportunities to save some cash you can find if you search them out.

Wow, The TV In This Place Is Huge!

An activity that is equally popular as a night out with friends, or a date, would be the humble trip to the cinema. Who doesn't love paying outrageous amounts for soft drinks and popcorn? The profit margin on cinema drinks is so incredibly high it boggles the mind. The price of a large Coke in McDonald's results in around 90% or more of the price you pay being pure profit. Given that cinemas make McDonald's drinks look incredibly cheap, you can imagine how much you are being fleeced every time you buy consumables at a cinema. As such, you are likely to want to save cash wherever you can when going to see a film.

If you're in the UK, an easy way to cut the cost of tickets in half is Orange Wednesdays. Orange offer their customers two for the price of one tickets on Wednesdays. Not an Orange customer? Not a problem. The codes are sent by text message, so the chances are at least one of your

12. Entertainment

friends will not be using theirs. Get them to get the code, and then forward the text to you. The main drawback of this is in the name. It's only available on Wednesday.

Perhaps the best way to save money at the cinema would be to see if the chain you visit has some sort of unlimited plan you can sign up for. Let's take the UK Cineworld chain as an example. According to the website, the standard price for a 2D film on their website is £8.70, with a 10% discount for booking online which brings it to £7.83.

If you are a regular visitor, you may want to consider the unlimited card they offer. For £14.99 a month you can go to as many showings of as many films as you like. In practice, you need to see at least 2 films a month, or 24 a year, to see any savings. Obviously the more you use it, the more you will save. Though any 3D films will require a small surcharge to be paid. It's worth pointing out that you also get 10% of any food and drink you buy.

The majority of their cinemas also have arrangements with local bars and restaurants that will see your unlimited card be worth discounts between 10%-50%. Finally, if you recommend a friend who signs up using your code, you both get a month for free. This can be done up to twelve times, so potentially a year of cinema free, if you can persuade twelve people to sign up of course.

Discounts like this are not limited to the UK. Wherever you live, there will be some sort of discount you can get. Those of you who happen to be in Portugal on a Monday can take advantage of Wonderful Monday. Monday isn't the day most of us associate with a trip to the cinema, but if you do go then you can get discounts on the entry price. While are a few cinemas who have decided they are too good for this, most places will help you keep the cost down on Mondays.

Those of you in Portugal who are customers of Zon Cable service can get buy one get one free on any visit to the cinema, due to their parent company being Lusomundo. Obviously this is only for Lusomundo cinemas, but not having to go on a Monday makes it far more flexible than the Wonderful Monday deal.

As you can see there are wonderful ways to save money everywhere without having to sit at home in the dark or reading library books by candlelight, straining your eyesight.

13. The Wonders Of Online Shopping

We know it might seem a little silly to do most of your shopping online but there are a few good reasons to actually do it. We are not recommending you become a shut in and start collecting your pee in jars in your fridge but you can go out for things that truly matter. Some types of stores are closing down anyway so your only bet might be buying things online. Most entertainment stores are closing down and almost everyone does their shopping for DVDs, Blu-Rays and video games online. If you still go to stores to buy these products you always risk the store having run out of stock or not even stocking that product. And in this new age of technology we don't know anyone who still enjoys the waiting period and going to a store time and time again to see if what they wanted has come in. But hey, some people are just weird.

Some of the advantages of doing your shopping online are:

- Saving money on gas (driving to and from the shop)
- A very large array of products to choose from
- Buying presents for acquaintances that live far away from you (those shops will ship to other addresses directly)
- Brands not normally available in your city or even country

13. The Wonders Of Online Shopping

- Buying directly from the country it was produced (a friend of ours bought a car part at one eighth of the price shops were selling at his home country)

First, make sure you are getting the best deal. If you visit a few different websites before clicking that "buy" button you will be pretty sure you are not paying a fortune for something that could cost a lot less at your corner shop.

Some banks have cards created specifically for online shopping. These cards have lower credit limits. With some of them you can even "deposit" money into whenever you want to purchase something online and that is your limit. If your credit card number ever gets stolen there isn't much money they can steal since they can only withdraw the money you actually put in there. These methods are very safe and a wonderful idea. So you get to buy that watch you always wanted and laugh at the people trying to get 5000 dollars from your account. Good luck with that. There are varying charges on these pre-paid cards though, make sure to shop around to get the best deal.

If your bank does not offer this type of credit cards, get one with a great insurance that you can claim fraud easily if you plan on using sketchy (non-standard) websites that you don't really trust. We do not advise on using these websites but hey, sometimes that phone cover on that website in Alaska really looks awesome, we understand if you want to get it (although if you're buying Hello Kitty phone covers from Japan we can't really help you there).

We can suggest a few trustworthy websites for you since we know most people worry a bit about the safety of inputting their credit card information online and having their hard-earned money stolen from them. We have been loyal customers for some of these websites for years on end and their customer service is brilliant, along with their shipping and postage.

DVDs, Blu-ray's, Games and Books

Amazon (www.amazon.co.uk or amazon.com)

Amazon, and sites like it, are a major factor in the decline of the entertainment megastores. You have at your disposal thousands or maybe millions of books, movies and video games, at the distance of a mouse click. It is extremely easy to use and they are very fast at answering questions from their customers, as well as shipping things to your home. We cannot recommend them enough. Sometimes they have products on sale and special deals which are unbeatable. One of our writers has even bought a treadmill from them and they shipped it to another country. An entire treadmill.

Play (www.play.com)

Play for us is the bastard brother of Amazon. It's not as pretty but sometimes they have great sales and they are very fast at shipping as well. If Amazon or Play do not have it, it means it does not exist.

Ebuyer (www.ebuyer.com)

For computers, computer parts, entertainment gear and

13. The Wonders Of Online Shopping

office equipment, this is where you should go. They are often the cheapest online for these types of products and good their customer service is normally excellent.

Clothing

Asos (www.asos.com)

Asos (As Seen On Screen) is the biggest and best online shopping store for clothing items. They represent hundreds of brands and they even have a little video on each item so you can see how it looks on a model (remember she is a model, maybe she does look good in that leopard leotard but you might not). They represent so many brands you're bound to find things that you could never buy in your hometown.

Deals

Hot UK Deals (www.hotukdeals.com)

They don't sell products but they post the best deals around so if you're willing to dig through it a little bit you will find very good prices that trustworthy websites are offering. These deals are posted by anyone who finds them, not the websites themselves, and they are often short term deal, so keep a regular eye on the site.

Travel

Expedia (www.expedia.com/co.uk)

If you want to book a trip you can do it the traditional way and book it through a travel agent or you can stop being lazy and do everything yourself. We have never found a travel agent that has gotten us a better price than us doing the "leg" (keyboard) work and booking everything ourselves. We have booked vacation packages but we mostly book separate airplanes and hotel rooms and look for the best deals. Expedia is pretty good for both actually and they have been around for years, you can trust your credit card and your first born with them. Look for "special deals" and keep your eyes open.

Hotels.com (www.hotels.com)

Stop being lazy and instead of getting a semi-OK vacation package with a dinky hotel room and a bad airline look for everything yourself. Hotels.com offers very good sales sometimes and shows you most of the hotels in the area you want to stay at.

TripAdvisor (www.tripadvisor.com)

After you have decided on a hotel, check TripAdvisor. You can even book your hotel through it, but TripAdvisor is mainly good for reading reviews from other travellers who have been to the hotel or destination you want to go to. You need to take everything with a grain of salt on this website because some travellers are very nitpicky (*"there was a SPECK of dust behind the television in my room, I am never ever going to stay in that chain again,*

13. The Wonders Of Online Shopping

disgusting!!"), while others are so relaxed about travelling they might not desire the same level of comfort you do (*"after I pushed away the roaches the bed was soft and clean and I slept very soundly"*). Just read through the reviews and see if it's a hotel you would like to stay in. They advise on the area where the hotel is located at, hygiene, transportation, everything you can think of. A few years ago we booked a hotel that had construction near it and other travellers warned us of this issue. We emailed the hotel directly and when we got there we had a very nice quiet room away from all the noise and a bottle of Champagne waiting for us.

Airline Websites (www.ba.com www.klm.com www.easyjet.com etc)

A few years ago airline websites had very expensive airline tickets but the world has changed and evolved and sometimes you can get the best flights by going directly to their website and booking. This way the airline is cutting the middleman and the associated expenses. It also makes managing your reservation that much easier, you can immediately choose a special meal if you want to, pre-choose the seats (if the company allows it) and insert traveller information if you are going to a destination that has that prerequisite.

We strongly suggest you subscribe to a few airline newsletters so you can know if they have a special sale going on. There is a lot of money to be saved when airlines want to fill airplanes at the lowest seasons of the year.

Booking in advance is also a very good idea as most

airlines make tickets available 330 days before the date. You should also sign up for any air miles type schemes with whoever you fly with.

As you can see the internet was made for making your life easier and not just for watching porn. You will save a lot of money if you take advantage of these websites.

A little word of warning, booking hotels and airplanes separately should only be used if you are going to a relatively safe place. It's fine to do this to European destinations, the US and Canada, Japan, etc. But if you are planning on an adventure in a country where you don't know the language and that can be known as being unsafe for tourists (like for example Egypt after the Arab Spring, Turkey, Afghanistan, Angola, who knows what strikes your fancy) you might want a vacation package that includes transportation and a travel agency with contacts in those countries that can help you in case you get into any trouble. We wouldn't want you to be kidnapped and then blame it on us because you were trying to find a nice cheap shuttle to take you to the hotel and you ended up in the scary black van with tinted windows and men with machine guns pointed at you.

Be safe while traveling, it's supposed to be a relaxing activity, not a life or death situation that involves ransom requests and you holding that day's newspaper.

Cashback When Shopping

Advertising online is widespread. Unless you have installed

13. The Wonders Of Online Shopping

some sort of ad blocker on your computer, you will be bombarded with them pretty much everywhere you go online. To most of us they are occasionally helpful, as they inform us of something we didn't know about, or remind us of something we have forgotten about. But for the most part they are just annoying. There are ways to make them work for you though.

Adverts are big business since massive amounts of money moves due to them. Most of the time, the only movement your own cash sees is outgoing, but what if you could change that?

The way most adverts work is that the site hosting them gets a cut of any sales generated by them. You see an advert for that film you have been meaning to buy. You click the advert, it takes you to Amazon, or wherever, and you buy the film. The site that displayed that advert gets a percentage of whatever you bought.

Wouldn't it be better if that percentage went to you and not some website? There are a load of sites that help you do this. The only one we have actually used though is Quidco, based in the UK, online at www.quidco.com

They have the adverts, though not displayed as such. You click their links to get to sites, you buy stuff, and the money that would normally be paid to the advertising site is paid to your Quidco account instead. The first £5 you make per year the site keeps, the rest is yours.

Here are some examples of what kind of cashback you could get by using the Quidco site. Keep in mind these examples are correct at the time of writing and may have gone down, or indeed up, from then.

Hotels.com – 10% on everything. If you book a hotel and the total cost is £200, you get £20 back.

Expedia.co.uk – 10% for hotel bookings. 1% for flights. 3.5% for holiday package deals. 7% for car rental. 12% for activities.

Sky TV & Broadband & Phone – Not a percentage, but a fixed price depending on what you order. Sky+ or Sky+HD subscriptions get you £100 back. Add broadband on top is another £15, Add talk unlimited phone package for another £5. Other offers also exist for other services; check the Quidco site for full details.

Apple Store – 2% for iPhone sales. 2% for iPad 2 sales, 1% for the iPad 3.

PC World – 10% for printers, scanners & software. 7% for laptops over £300. 1.5% for all other sales including iPads and other tablets.

Play.com – 6% for clothing and accessories. 4% for gifts and gadgets. 2% for CD's, DVD's, books & games.

Netflix - £5 cashback for a new customer completing a free trial. Yes, they will pay you to use the free trial. This rises to £20 if after the free trial you become a paying member. £20 is just under the cost of 3 months of Netflix in the UK.

13. The Wonders Of Online Shopping

Groupon – 5% of all sales. So not only the massive Groupon discount, but an additional 5% back of what little you did pay as well.

This is by no means an exhaustive list, there are many more places that you can buy from and get cashback.

While Quidco requires you to be a UK resident, there are ways around that. They do not ask for an address during sign up, and while they used to require a UK bank account, they now will make payments to a PayPal account. If you are somewhere in Europe and often shop on UK sites, you should give it a go. The worst that might happen is they don't pay you.

We would advise setting up a new Paypal account and seeing if you can get a UK friend to let you use their address as a delivery address on the Paypal account. That way if they actually bother to look and see what address you have on the Paypal account, they will see a UK address, though there is no requirement to attach an address for basic functionality. This probably won't be needed though.

There are many other ways to use the Internet to your advantage like this. You should always assume you can get a better deal elsewhere and search it out. A little leg work can often see you get a better deal!

14. Investments

Those of you lucky enough to have some spare cash will most likely keep it in the bank. Savings accounts are the method most of us, who aren't considered rich, use to store our extra cash. We earn interest on the cash deposited in such accounts, and depending on where you live; there are often some schemes which allow some of your savings to be used in such a way that provides tax free returns. An example would be an ISA (Individual savings account) in the UK.

These are accounts that allow a certain amount to be saved, and earn interest tax-free. That's all well and good, everyone likes tax-free earnings, but recent events have shown that banks can and do fail.

Stocks and shares are another common method of investing your money. However while this is officially an investment, given the risk involved, we feel it should be classified as gambling. Returns are not guaranteed and when the economy enters a rough patch, the chances are the stock market will see many people lose a lot of money.

So how do you invest your cash? What method gives the best return? The unfortunate answer is that there is no such thing as a guaranteed return. However there are a few things that over the long term are pretty unlikely to see you lose your savings. And we will also present some crazier

14. Investments

suggestions that may pay off brilliantly in the future for next to no outlay now.

Oil

You hear about the price of oil a lot. While it fluctuates, the trend in the price is unmistakably upwards. The fact that it is a finite resource means that, unless the world suddenly comes up with a method to reduce its reliance on fossil fuels, the demand for oil is not going away. The available stocks become scarcer and therefore cost more and more to extract.

Let's say that you had bought 1.000 barrels of oil in the year 2000, at a price of approximately $27. This would have cost you $27,000. Now had you put this into a savings plan offering 5% interest, and that interest level was fixed, in 2012 you would have $48,488.12

If you had bought the oil, and sold it at current prices, the result would be you would have around $93,000.

A far better return on your money.

Balloons!

While oil looks good, we believe there is a better option to sink your cash into. Helium. Yes, the stuff that goes in balloons to the delight of children everywhere.

You see Helium, like oil, is a finite resource. We do not have a way to synthesize it. When it's gone, it's gone, and that day is coming quicker than you might think.

Troikapocalypse

Let's look at some backstory. Helium is created by two methods that we know of. The nuclear fusion process inside stars, and the slow radioactive decay of terrestrial rocks. It cannot be manufactured by any means we know of. The world's supply of this noble gas came as a by-product of natural gas extraction.

The largest storage facility of Helium is in America. By 1995 one billion cubic meters of Helium were stored in the National Helium Reserve, a group of mines, pipes and vats in an underground region stretching over 200 miles from Amarillo, in Texas, to Kansas. This constituted over half of the Helium on the Earth.

Now while most people think of balloons at the mention of Helium, that is by no means its only, or most important, use. Some of the more important uses for the gas are as follows.

Telescopes - Not the kind you use to spy on the neighbours, the kind that are used by scientists in the massive telescopes in scientific observatories. Also in space-based telescopes. Helium is used to reduce the distorting effects of temperature variations between the lenses.

Rockets - Helium is used to condense oxygen and hydrogen in rocket fuel, to force fuel into engines during rocket launches, to pressurise liquid fuelled rockets and to clean out reusable rocket engines. NASA is one of the biggest users of Helium on the planet, and they make no attempt at all to recycle any of the Helium they use.

14. Investments

Cooling - Thanks to its low boiling point, liquid helium is used as coolant in many different fields. Infrared detectors, nuclear reactors, wind tunnels, satellites and spacecraft, MRI machines and the large hadron collider. All need liquid helium or they simply do not function.

By now you are probably asking yourself, "Why do they keep talking about Helium?" Well it's because in around 30 years, there won't be any left.

In 2006 the US Congress passed the Helium Privatization Act. This meant that the entire National Helium Reserve should be sold by 2015, irrespective of market prices. This has made Helium incredibly cheap to keep up with the schedule for getting rid of it all. The price had to come down. Way down.

It is estimated that if the market were to price Helium according to supply and demand, a helium balloon would need to cost around $100 since the scarcity of the gas would be taken into account. The actions of the American government have seen the price crash in response to all the helium they are dumping into the market.

If you have any spare cash, you should look into buying a load of this gas, and resist the temptation to put it in balloons or inhale it to make yourself talk funny. It won't be that far in the future when its rarity will mean it will fetch a massive price. Helium could potentially make the profits from oil look like pocket change.

If we take a longer view of investments, there are many

things that, with a little care and luck, could see you cash in later in life, or in some cases, provide nicely for your kids or grandkids down the line. Most of these things you wouldn't normally think of as investments. Collectables you see don't start life that way, they turn into that many years later.

Comic Books

Seen by many as a childish distraction, comic books can turn out to be worth quite a bit of money a few decades down the line. Just in case, treat them like they are now. Keep them sealed in bags with backboards. A large collection doesn't need to take up a lot of space if properly stored and if you are lucky, one day they might be worth more than your car, or possibly even your home.

The most expensive comic ever sold was a mint condition copy of Action Comics #1. It was released in June 1938 costing 10 cents and in November 2011 was sold for $2.16 million. While this is the absolute top of the scale, even newer comics can be worth quite a lot.

A near mint copy of Amazing Spiderman #1 from 1963 could fetch around $55,000 and a near mint copy of Iron Man #1 from 1968 being easily worth $5,000.

The lesson is clear, if you are going to read comics, treat them well! If you see a new series, buy the number 1 at least. You might be very glad you did someday.

Coins

14. Investments

How much is a penny worth? Normally the answer would be that a penny is worth a penny. This is not always the case though. If the penny in question is a 1943 bronze Lincoln penny, then it's actually worth $1.7 million.

Coin collections are easy. You find a coin that doesn't look like its spent months in a sewer, you keep it. It's not going to pay off now, or anytime soon, but in years to come, with a little luck, it might be worth something. More accurately, it might be worth more than the face value. Keep an eye out for any coins have different designs from normal. These pop up a lot, and they are often minted in far smaller numbers than the regular ones. As an example, in 1992 the UK produced a 50 pence coin to commemorate the finalisation of the European Community (as it was known then) into a single market, along with the British presidency of the same.

109,000 of these coins were produced. This might seem like a lot, but 5 years later when the 50 pence coin was redesigned to be smaller, half a billion of them were made. One of those coins in mint condition is already worth around £10.

Many countries also sell commemorative sets of coins, or single coins. These often do very well in terms of the value they gain over the years.

Video Games

Video games can also, unexpectedly, prove to be rather valuable down the line. Think twice before you trade that terrible game in for next to nothing as one day it could be worth a fair bit of money.

Do you remember the Sega Master System? It was the first console they produced which saw a worldwide release. It first arrived in stores in 1986 in the USA and 1987 in Europe. It was the system that first brought us Sonic the Hedgehog.

While the European version of this game is still rather easy to get your hands on, the American release is not. An American cartridge is nowadays worth around $400. The only way to differentiate the two versions is a code on the box, so you if you only have the cartridge, you probably won't be able to cash in. James "Buster" Douglas knockout boxing on the Master System is also rare enough that $200-$400 is the price it commands now.

The Nintendo Entertainment System, or NES as it is more commonly known, also has its share of valuable cartridges floating around. None more so than the cartridges used in the Nintendo World Championship & Nintendo Campus Challenge competitions. The gold cartridges from the 1990 world championship fetch around $20,000!

It doesn't always matter if a game is actually any good or not. Active Enterprises, seeing how popular the turtles were, created the Cheetahmen game. It was bad. Inexplicably, they decided to make a second one. There weren't many copies made, and it is generally considered to be one of the worst games ever made. However, that doesn't change the fact that owners of this game can expect

14. Investments

to get around $2,500 for it. There are many other NES games that easily fetch over $200.

A more recent system that almost everyone will be familiar with is the original Microsoft Xbox. While it is only around 10 years old, there is already a growing collection of games that will fetch over $100. Marvel Vs Capcom 2 goes for about $200.

It is worth considering whether you should trade in the games that can charitably be called crap, or if you should pack them up nicely and wait for the day when they are able to pay for a new car.

15. Stuck in Job Purgatory?

There is a growing number of young people that despite being highly qualified, motivated and extremely likely to be successful in the future, are currently on standby in job purgatory.

This is the generation that is taking jobs for which they are overqualified and probably only short-term roles that have zero relation to their field of expertise or study.

What Caused This?

As a consequence of the on-going financial crisis, when the job market started to sink the people that were last hired were often the first ones to be let go.

Due to the financial burdens that these workers accumulated to obtain their degrees such as student loans and bill payments, many were forced to apply and accept jobs that were outside their area and even goals. The short term objective is to survive until that dream job appears - but it most likely never will.

The Consequences?

15. Stuck in Job Purgatory?

Fact: One in five women are currently working part-time jobs

The US Department of Labour stated that in 2012 one in five women are working part-time because they cannot find full time work. Prior to the recession, that number was less than one in ten.

Financial obligations have forced women to take jobs for which they are overqualified. These are smart, ambitious and qualified women that find themselves with anxiety attacks, calluses or having to enrol the help of mental health specialists to deal with the consequences of not following their dreams.

Regardless of how unaffected some people are, most young people, male or female, are a generation of overeducated, "underemployed" lost souls.

This is not only affecting their work life but home life as well. According to a report carried out by the *Pew Research Centre* called "*Young, Underemployed and Optimistic*" all the factors mentioned above have contributed for what has now been labelled as the "*Boomerang Generation*". The recession stereotype of "*moving back in with the parents*" is unfortunately something that most of them will have to go through.

According to the Pew report about the US in 2010, 21.6% of respondents lived in a multi-generational household (this is a fancy way of saying you live with your mommy and daddy), which is a number that has gone up from

Troikapocalypse

15.8% in 2000. The share of 25 to 34 year-olds living in these conditions was at its lowest in 1980, when it was at about 11% and has risen steadily since the recession started in 2007.

But living with your parents isn't as bad as you think. It has some positive aspects you might be overlooking, such as:

1. If you live with your parents you will probably not have to do dishes every night, for everything you eat, entirely by yourself. If you are lucky your parents might even own a dishwasher - the magical device that you will always dream of having in your own home.

2. Your fridge will stop looking like you live off beer, coke and frozen meals. Your family will have fresh fruit, vegetables and all sorts of things you never remember to pick up from the supermarket. Also, you are all sharing the bills which brings living expenses down. That is why you can stop eating things directly from a can.
3. Also: hot food appears, as if by magic, on a plate. This is the type of food that would take you up to two hours to cook but your mom magically appears to whip up out of nothing.

4. If you live on your own you will understand the responsibilities associated to being the only living being in a property. If you own pets they have to be walked and you are the only person around for that. If your house needs maintenance guess who needs to stay home and babysit the repair man? If an important package arrives, most

15. Stuck in Job Purgatory?

likely you will have to go to the post office to pick it up. Living with other people allows you to divide these chores.

5. Everything is always super clean! Unless your family is a hoarder nightmare, most families are tidy and clean which means that the communal areas of your parents' house will most likely be spotless without you having to do all the work.

6. Bills. Do we need to say more? Living on your own is expensive. You can help yourself and your parents by helping out with their financial responsibilities.

7. Nice toys that your parents bought over the years that you cannot afford on your own. Nothing like sitting in front of a huge TV with 5.1 Dolby surround - even if you have to share it.

8. If you are feeling sick you will have your family around you so you can stay in bed all day while your mommy can bring you soup and toast.

9. Laundry: Your mom never mentioned this but laundry is like being stuck in the Twilight Zone or the movie Groundhog Day. It's a never ending cycle of things getting dirty, clean and then dirty again. At your parents you have a magically filled wardrobe where things appear more organized and actually folded. Your wardrobe will stop looking like it's an endless pile of t-shirts that have been rolled up and just thrown in there.

10. Your parents' home will probably be filled with food treats and things you cannot afford on your own.

11. If you are unemployed and living on your own you might sink into a pit of despair and even have difficulty leaving the house. Seeing active grown people around you will motivate you to get out of the house, even if it's only to help your mother with the groceries or go walk the dog in the park.

12. When you are away from your personal space you do not have the same tendency to make stupid mistakes like staying up to play your PlayStation 3 until the sun comes up. Having your parents walk up to you in their pyjamas at 3am to give you the dirty look of shame might make you realize you are not sixteen years old anymore.

13. When you live on your own having a whole dessert for dinner seems to be a viable option. This is not the case when you live with other people.

And last, but not least:

14. Realizing your family is amazing, that they love you and dedicated many years of their life to raise you. When you get older and stop being a stupid teen you can finally open your eyes to see how much they care (thank you mom and dad!)

You get the point. Yes, you lose privacy and you cannot take people home with you and hang out with your friends. But having a place to stay when you run out of options is a modern world commodity that should not be taken for granted.

16. Pimp Your Life

As you are already aware there are people out there who work as life coaches. Life coaching is a practice that helps people achieve personal goals by using a set of tools and techniques.

We are not against this practice. Hell, we probably need it ourselves. We do however think that there are a couple of things you can try before you take out your wallet and pay someone for this service. Leave the difficult things for the life coach professionals but try these simple tips to "pimp your life". They will help you at home, find a job and who knows, maybe even world domination.

Enjoy Your Home Life

A trick to be happier at work is to actually have a happy life at home. Yes, work can feel like you are stuck in Hell, but if your home life makes you happy you will have a smile on your face as soon as you walk out that cubicle. Enjoy the time with your family and make your home life more exciting. You might not have any money but it doesn't mean you need to get stuck in the same routine every day.

How about playing random games with your family? Before your significant other arrives home with the kids, get some toy pistols (these can be water pistols if you do not mind getting your home a bit wet) and leave them in a

16. Pimp Your Life

visible place with a note. Let your family know that you have the other toy gun and that the game starts now. Plan themed nights such as Mexican dinner day and Superhero adventures cooking night. You'll be a hero to your kids if they find you cooking wearing a pirate hat and an eye patch.

Get Organized

Another thing you need to do is to get organized. If your home life is organized, you will feel more relaxed and this will improve your chances of having a more successful work life.

Try to keep important information at home organized in different folders that are easily accessible, clutter free and clearly labelled. Do not store unnecessary documentation that you will not use.

Create ring-binders/folders for:
- A current year binder with sections for all your yearly files. These sections should hold your taxes, water, gas and electricity bills, different insurances, medical expenses etc. Once the year finishes you should start a brand new folder for the new year and keep this one for tax and other purposes.
- A generic folder with information on your current contracts like rental contracts, banking, insurances, etc.
- A work and education folder that holds your documentation, work contracts, recommendation letters and diplomas. Add a copy of your resume for safekeeping in case you lose the electronic file.

Once all your paperwork is organized it will be much easier to find things when you need it. Whenever you have to find that bill from 6 months ago it will be at hand's reach.

Digital Organization

You should also keep your digital life organized. Your home computer should hold easily accessible copies of your information and scans of essential information recruiters and future job employers might ask of you. Try to keep everything sorted into folders and avoid easy mistakes like leaving things on the desktop just because it is useful. If your computer crashes this data might never be recovered and you will never remember to make backups.

Trick: if you use numbers when naming your folders they will be organized by number instead of by name. This is useful when you want to keep your own logic to find things quickly.

If you start creating folders such as, for example, "Bills", "CVs", "Scans", "My Files", "Temporary Files" and "Other Files", you will very likely in the future start filling random files under incorrect folders. Does a scan of a letter of recommendation get filled under "Scans" or should it be moved to the "CVs" folder? These small decisions might seem trivial but after a couple of years of this you will be dreading the day you gave your folders such generic names. If you keep things crisp clear, you will ensure a clutter free computer.

You can try a folder organization like the following:

16. Pimp Your Life

01. Education
        01. Certificates
        02. Scans
        03. Projects and Coursework
02. Work Applications and CVs
        01. Documentation scans
        02. Cover Letters
        03. CVs
        04. Recommendation Letters
03. Work
        01. Job 1
        02. Job 2
04. Holidays
        01. Receipts
        02. Useful Information
05. Financial
        01. Bank Statements
        02. Tax Information
06. Photos
        01. Holidays
        02. Family Photos
(etc.)

But What About The Content?

Trick: If you number files with a "year-month-date" format before the actual name of the file you can keep them permanently organized regardless of the amount of files.

This is extremely useful if you need to create several updated of a CV or an important work file and you want to make sure you always access the latest copy.

For example, if you have a "my cv.doc" and "my cv 2.doc" and "my cv latest copy.doc" besides looking extremely unprofessional and chaotic, you might end up getting confused and using an old copy of the file. Do you really want to send your possible future employer that CV copy from two years ago that you have re-worked a dozen times and corrected at least four different spelling errors? If you number and date your files to look something similar to "2011 03 - John Smith CV.doc" and "2012 06 - John Smith CV.doc" not only does it look more organized but you also know right away which one is the latest copy.

Back Everything Up

We have all gone through this. One day you get home, you sit in front of your laptop, press a button, and nothing works. Or even worse, you get the Windows blue screen of death.

We all know who is to blame here. No, it's not Microsoft, it's you. Why didn't you just get a USB or an external hard disk and did a backup of all of your files?

Lots of new technologies and systems out there now allow you to back up your important files online, like for example Google Drive, Microsoft Skydrive and Dropbox. It's a good idea to keep copies online where you can access them everywhere and where you're pretty sure that if your country gets nuked by an angry neighbour and your beloved computers all get fried by an EMP (electromagnetic pulse), you can still think "Haha you idiots, I stored all my pornographic photos online! I might

16. Pimp Your Life

have forgotten all my important bank information and scans of my personal documents but the angry rants I wrote about my coworkers are still safe".

Once you get your life organized you can move on to actually organizing your work life (your CV should be representative of this) and your cover letter should tell people about you, how amazing you are and how together your life is, even if it isn't.

Google Yourself

Before sending out CVs with your name and contact information you should always remember that your Internet presence will haunt you and make people form opinions that might not always be true. If you have a particular name that is not very common this is even more important since googling your name will probably return some results which are directly connected to you.

So always do the simple exercise of googling your name and email address to see what comes up. it might sound strange, but if you find that you get results that you would prefer not to be shown to your professional contacts, you might need to take some actions such as changing email address, closing down social networking sites, changing profile privacy settings, etc.

Does googling your personal email address return an old account for a particular sex forum you do not want people to know about? Might be time to create a new "clean" email account.

The Anatomy Of The Cover Letter

We have all read those pesky job ads that ask for your CV, a cover letter and a signed copy of your will. We have all rolled our eyes at having to write a personalized cynical letter describing how much we love said company, although we never had really heard about them before, how licking stamps and cleaning toilets all day would fulfil all our career objectives and how amazing and excited you are over this average and amazingly low paid opportunity.

Fortunately for us we can dissect a cover letter and make everyone's lives much simpler.

The opening sentence should be used to introduce yourself and state your expensive degree from a not even remotely known university where you studied your much loved but useless major.

In the next paragraph you should provide a believable reason why this job is everything you are looking for in (insert random industry) and how much you would love to work for (insert name of company you had to Google to know what they actually do).

This is where your degree will come in handy since you will need to use some big words that will make it look like you know what you are doing. Words such as "synergy", "passion", "methodology", "organization", "entrepreneurship", "social awareness", "high value outcome", "core skills", "leadership", "corporate values" and "strategic staircase". Explain how your "technical

16. Pimp Your Life

skills" and "valued experience" will be an "important asset" to (insert company name).

The next section is important since you will be listing your most relevant or recent unpaid internship, crap job and/or hobby that you have renamed to make it sound more important. You should explain your current situation (remember, you are are not unemployed, you are between jobs or exploring other career opportunities) and you should finish the paragraph with an impressive statistic and how you achieved a goal or dream.

Onwards and you should explain how organized and amazing you are, the high standards that distinguish you from other people and how you managed to achieve something against all odds (no, not killing your annoying colleague in your last job is not an achievement here). If you provide an additional challenge that you had to overcome it should show your "work ethic", "detail orientation", "punctuality", "teamwork" and "professionalism". If you can get "emotional intelligence" in that sentence it will give you extra brownie points.

In addition to everything you wrote before, you should use the keywords they used in their job description and reiterate that you are a leader/team player and provide an example of something you accomplished in your life. Were you in the boy scouts? Go on, find a way of adding it on there.

The next paragraph should mention all the stuff that your employer will attempt to squash by treating you like a slave for the next twenty years. Tell them that you have enthusiasm, a sense of humour and soft communication skills.

Unfortunately you are not a snowflake, but regardless of the truth, your next paragraph should mention how unique you are and provide a generic statement about the strong connection with (insert company name here). Tell them as well how they can get a hold of you (details at the top of the page) but avoid directing them to your Facebook or Twitter handle.

Don't forget to thank them for their patience, consideration and for them taking the time to reach the end of your letter. Explain how excited you are at the chance of applying to the specified role and just for the chance of being considered (you should feel like a candidate to the Miss World Pageant here).

Finish off with something professional and cold such as "Sincerely" or "Kind regards".

Rinse and repeat.

Curriculum Vitae: What To Avoid

Some of the examples we are going to present to you right now will make you think we are lying and just making things up for laughs. But we are not. When you know people that work in Human Resources that have heard and seen it all you get to hear some amusing stories. So we have decided to present to you a short collection of things you should avoid including in your CV and job applications.

16. Pimp Your Life

Bible-Sized CVs And Applications

Seriously? You have a ten page CV? Good luck with getting any recruiter to read more than two pages of that. Usually recruiters, mainly in harsh times like an economic crisis, go through dozens, if not hundreds, of CVs per day. Sometimes they work with such tight deadlines to fill a job position that finding any candidate is more important than finding the right candidate which means that will read diagonally as many CVs as possible.

Having your information in an organized and concise format is crucial so that a recruiter knows immediately you are the one they are looking for.

You will have a later chance, if you make it to the interview part of the recruitment process, to explain in detail what you did in your previous roles, the impact you made, what makes you the best and why they should hire you. But to get to this milestone you need to get your CV quickly noticed by someone you might not be an expert on the area you work in. So having crucial key words recruiters are looking for clearly visible for the eye to see is key.

Let's try a quick test:

Example 1:

Job Description: Five years experience as a Database Developer in a Consultancy company in a Customer Relationship Management project with key stakeholder sponsorship. Responsible for the creation of a customer database with special attention to the Extraction, Transformation and Loading of transaction data and data mining requirements as defined by the functional processes.

Example 2

Job Description:
- Database Developer with 5 Years experience
- CRM Project in a Consultancy company
- Customer database development with ETL requirements

So which one did you read faster and got the point across more efficiently? Example number 2 saves you space, is direct and straight to the point and summarizes in less than 3 lines what Example 1 aims to explain in 7 lines.

Another CV No No - Useless Information

Another shocking thing people have included in their CV is their favourite colour or even their zodiac sign. Why, you ask us? We don't know. It's a mystery.

Another heart wrenching mistake people do is think that just because you are using a computer with access to at least several million colour levels you need to try to use all of them to make your CV look amazing. It does not. It makes it look like you have either discovered that you can actually change the font colour or you have asked your five-year old to help you. Also, the type of letter font you select is important. Comic Sans MS? Are you applying to

16. Pimp Your Life

work at an ice-cream shop? You might as well use heart-shaped stickers everywhere.

Our advice here is to keep your CV in grey scale or to a maximum of 3 colours. It will look more professional and be more printer friendly.

One of our recruiter friends once saw a CV written in light grey with lime green and yellow sections. She compared it with trying to look directly into the sun. Surely she remembers it, but not the content or if that person got the job which, is kind of, the whole point.

Now, onto the sensitive subject of photos. We have discussed this topic in much detail (ok, maybe not a lot of detail... we had a beer and the topic came up for 20 seconds) and it is clear that opinions differ over the inclusion, or not, or a photo in your CV.

Believe it or not, it appears that some people actually include a full body A4 sized photo attached to their CV. This, obviously, made us laugh out loud for some time which made writing this chapter very difficult. We thought about including a full sized photo of us, your wonderful authors, laughing hysterically like a bunch of hyenas but since we want to keep our publishing price quite low (there is a crisis out there, haven't you heard?) we have decided against it.

So we can conclude that it is incredibly ridiculous to include a full sized photo of yourself. On the other hand, if you are quite attractive and have a nice smile you should include your photo since that will make your CV pop out in the sea of hundreds of people that are now applying to every job in the world.

You should always try to make the photo itself seem professional: dress nicely, brush your hair, put some makeup on - but avoid looking like a streetwalker or a clown. Either take a photo booth photo, a professional one or even ask a friend to take an instant snap. Avoid using random photos of you on a night out or on a beach somewhere. It might be ok for Facebook, but they do not demonstrate professionalism.

Also avoid using that nice photo that shows how big your breasts are or that college photo of you doing shots, unless you are applying to an exotic dancer or bartender position. In that case it might be a requirement.

Whilst on the photo subject we can quickly address the CV size issue. When using a digital CV and photo you can control the size of the file you are sending by adding a smaller sized photo and converting your file to a PDF format. This will have two benefits: the first one is that the recruiter will not be able to make "small changes" to your cv just because they are desperate and think that replacing "Basic Knowledge" with "Expert" is not that big of a change. The second benefit is that you will not be annoying everyone, from the recruiter to your future boss, with a 10Mb CV that will clog everyone's Outlook account.

Last but not least, we have contact details. You should always include your Country address and your phone contacts with an international dialling number when you are sending out international job applications (+44 (0)

16. Pimp Your Life

xxxxxxxxxx for example). Your email address is also extremely important and that email that you created back when you were 15 is probably not appropriate. "Sxybuny69" might not be the best message you want to portray to your future employers.

What To Include

So we have given you a large list of things to avoid and to consider. So what are the tricks of the trade that will help you get noticed?

Our first advice is to include a summary section at the top of the first page of your CV. This short section should have a maximum of 5 to 6 lines, probably should be in a box or some sort of delimitation to make it look different from the rest of the file and should include one sentence of what you have done such as "Over 10 years' experience in the Flower Arrangement industry". It should include your highest level of education like "Graduated with honours from Hogwarts School of Magic" and should state what you are doing now and what you are looking for in a job and in the future like, for example, "I am currently working as a full time secretary in a Fortune 500 company and I am looking for a role that will fulfil my dreams of helping other people in their moments of sadness and happiness by creating beautiful flower bouquets for weddings and funerals".

See? In a few words we have an insight of the motivation behind the job application.

Show Them That You Have The X-Factor

Regarding your actual CV content, you should try to find that one obscure fact that makes you unique. For example, if you are really good at math you should probably make a point of adding this to your CV. If you really enjoy collecting packets of sugar, you can probably leave it out.

Let's provide you with an example. We have a friend that stated that one of the authors involved in writing this book had "scary googling skills" (we are not telling you which one!). This was due to the fact that when this person was saying that the internet did not have that much stored information on an individual person or that it was difficult to find, one of us went on a quest to prove this person wrong and ended up finding a blog post from a family member back in 2006 with photos of a family party. This was widely available to anyone with an internet connection and that person's email address. This skill to find obscure information sounds scary, but anyone can do this.

The truth is that most of us use this to our advantage every day at work. Whenever we have an issue we Google for answers first and only afterwards do we look for answers amongst our peers. This makes us independent. When searching for answers we sometimes discover new things that we were not looking for in the first place.

A Wall Street Journal survey of corporate human resources and leadership-development professionals identified "*strategic thinking*" as the business skill most sought by companies. What does this mean? It means that in order to realize our full potential, we must embrace what makes us unique.

16. Pimp Your Life

You should ask yourself what are the activities that make you different from other people or what characteristics and traits that make you unique.

Lying: The New Art Of CV Writing

We all know people that do this, people that constantly get away with lying in their CV. Who doesn't know a friend that changed the dates from his degree to hide that year that was wasted partying or that job that was a mistake since day one?

We have also heard news stories about famous people who have done it as well, such as the CEO of Yahoo that in May 2012 was forced to resign after it was discovered that his CV should be filed under "fiction" instead of "boardroom material".

We have identified six areas of deceit that are used in CV cheating and we are providing some famous examples. Although these examples show that sometimes liars do reach the top, they also demonstrate that you can get caught and ridiculed.

1. Fake Education

Most job advertisements nowadays demand you to have a minimum education requirement to apply. Even lower paid jobs are asking for a Degree (nothing like scrubbing a toilet with your Masters diploma). It doesn't actually mean that you have to remember what you studied, which you probably won't since your vodka fuelled nights have blurred out that part of your life. All that matters is that you have a piece of paper stating that you were committed to something for X years and finished it.

It appears that whilst some of us have spent years and a lot of brain cells trying to get that paper sent in before the deadline, others have decided that studying is for suckers and that having a degree is just a question of picking a University and deciding which level of education you want with no effort whatsoever.

Famous example: Dr. Laura Callahan had been a Deputy Chief Information Officer for the US Department of Labor. She had a Ph.D. in Computer Science, amongst many other degrees. In reality, all her degrees had been purchased from the internet within the space of a year and she had backdated them to make it all appear real. This wouldn't be a problem if she did not hold one of the most important IT positions in the US as the Department of Homeland Security's Deputy Chief Information Officer when she got caught. Nothing like having a liar with full access to all the sensitive, private and national security information of one of the world's most important superpowers.

2. Fake Experience

The "Work Experience" section in your CV forms the essential core for all Human Resources personnel to judge you and know if you will have success in your future. It includes dates, job titles, descriptions and, if you are lucky, ways you actually contributed to help your previous employer.

16. Pimp Your Life

In today's competitive reality it is highly likely you have jumped from company to company to achieve better remuneration for your work (admit it, you are a modern job mercenary). But unfortunately this is not seen as something positive from your future employers. They will think you are flaky and that you have "loyalty issues". Due to this, some people will probably decide to move dates around and try to hide time gaps.

Some people do take this to a whole other level and think that creating a CV is like writing a novel, building a character and a whole new life to take them where they want to go. Of course, you cannot just say you have invented the wheel or the Internet, that is just too obvious.

Famous example: Highly decorated retired Lt. Col. Jay Cafasso worked for Fox News as an expert "military and counter-terrorism consultant" during their coverage of the invasion of Afghanistan. The truth? His only military experience was in 1976 and he was discharged only after 44 days of boot camp.

3. Fake Skills

This is the fluffiest, most subjective, part of a CV. What exactly is a skill? A skill is what you will bring to the job. So, in theory, it should be just a bunch of keywords that get picked up by job filters and robots that are a part of the hiring process.

Since there is a high probability of you getting tested on your skills in the interview process, if you try to bullshit your way through this section, you will very likely get caught in the first ten seconds of the test. Nothing like looking like a deer in headlights when someone asks you a basic question on a topic that you are an "expert" of.

Famous example: As president of IBM's Lotus Development Corp. unit. Jeffrey Papows was the Chuck Norris of the Nerd world. His past experience and skills were as noble as they were badass. From a lonely orphan child he went to become a daring Marine pilot, with a black belt in tae kwon do and a Ph.d. from Pepperdine University. He also was a compassionate soul that, after surviving a F4 Phantom jet crash, helped support the widow of his fellow pilot who died ejecting from the same doomed jet. Fortunately for at least two people, he wasn't an orphan and everything else was bullshit as well. Shame on you nerd Chuck Norris. Shame. On. You.

4. Fake Identity

One would assume that your name, the thing that defines who you are, would be the last thing that people would fake on their CV. But it does happen.

Now before you go and change your name to "Steve Jobs" and apply for a job at Apple, maybe you should stop and think. If you would indeed get hired, you would have to live your entire working life under that assumed name.

Famous example: In the mid-1970s Gerald Barnbaum, a pharmacist who lost his license due to Medicaid fraud charges, legally changed his last name to Barnes in order to become Dr. Gerald C. Barnes, a respected orthopaedic surgeon living in Stockton, California. He embarked on a 20-year career of impersonating the real doctor through obtaining copies of the real doctors diplomas and credentials. Barnbaum was caught and imprisoned five times between 1979 and 2004. He is now serving his fifth prison sentence, a 10-year term on fraud charges and an additional 2 and a half years for the escape he pulled during his 4th sentence - in which he tried to resume work as Dr. Barnes.

5. Fake References

Once you get deeper into the interviewing process, references become incredibly important. When hiring for a position of any responsibility, most hiring managers will check up on at least a couple references for their chosen candidates. And if everyone who ever worked with you is glad they get to use the past tense of "work" then you could be in a lot of trouble.

Famous example: Adam Wheeler reached his senior year at Harvard University before anyone found out that he falsified his credentials in order to get in. He fabricated letters of recommendation from numerous professors at Harvard, where he used writing samples that were plagiarized from other professors and his CV included a list of books that he supposedly co-authored, and lectures and courses he supposedly taught. In May of 2010 Wheeler was indicted on twenty counts, including identity fraud and larceny.

6. Fact Exaggeration

As Nick Isles from the UK Institute of Personnel and Development stated "The majority of job applications involve if not outright lies, certainly exaggerations". Job seekers are not only lying but also embellishing their experience to make it look more impressive. The most common areas of misrepresented information are academic qualifications, remuneration and interests. Since most of us have fairly uninteresting hobbies and interests, embellishing a little bit is sort of understandable. Some people take exaggeration to a whole other level however.

Famous example: Yahoo's CEO, Scott Thompson alleged credentials included bachelor's degrees in Accounting and Computer Science. In reality he only had a degree in Accounting but somehow, over the years, "Computer Science" sort of grew into Thompson's CV.

You are probably thinking that the examples above have nothing to do with the crisis. You need to remember that these are people in power, pretending to be doctors that make life or death decisions, CEOs dictating the future, companies that employ thousands of people, or role models to impressionable teens that will learn that being dishonest is normal.

For each example above of someone that got caught lying, there are probably hundreds of even thousands of scammers, liars and bullshitters that have gotten away with it. And some of them are now in positions of power, such as politicians, CEOs, consultants or experts. These are the people that are deciding what happens to us and the generations to come. Shocked? Yes, so are we.

16. Pimp Your Life

We are not saying don't lie on your CV, just make sure you are able to live up to whatever wild claims you make!

17. The Idiot's Guide To Job Hunting

How to make it look like you know what you are doing

Career Advice Companies

If you do not know what a career advice company is you can skip this chapter, it probably means you either do not need them or you are successful at marketing yourself. These companies, very much like fashion advisors and personal shoppers, try to advise you on what to include in your CV (curriculum vitae, or resume, call it whatever you want), what jobs you should be applying to, what is your best career move at the time. They will also help you connect to closed circles of head hunters that you probably never would have had access to. Unlike a personal shopper, you cannot change your skills and experience by owning a nice pair of shoes and a fancy suit. A career is something personal that dominates most of our lives and should not be decided by someone that you are paying money to.

Unless you are a complete zero at selling yourself and writing up your CV or you have a lot of money to spend, you can probably go without a career helper just by following a few simple rules. What we are trying to say is that you should not be paying someone else to tell you how to best present yourself since you know yourself much

17. The Idiot's Guide To Job Hunting

better than anyone else. And who best to know what jobs you should be after then the person who might end up doing them, right?

Of course, you should ask your colleagues, bosses, friends and family to give you some personal input since most of these people might actually like you and want to help out, although it might be best for you to refrain from asking advice from your manager or boss if you are looking for a new job and still working at your previous one. From personal experience, bosses hate traitors, quitters and wussy employees that have a mercenary perspective on life.

Linkedin

This little website, although filled with annoying self-marketers that think that having a douchebag photo in a suit and 2,000 connections make them look really successful, is actually one of the best recruitment tools out there.

A lot of head-hunters and recruitment companies are increasing their online presence and LinkedIn appears to be the best one in this type of website. Large companies such as Google, Microsoft, Fortune 500 companies, consultancy companies, amongst many others, are regularly posting jobs and international opportunities on the "Jobs" section of the site, and head-hunters are always lurking the specialist groups searching for the best candidates out there.

To make this more tempting, it is really simple to create a

profile for free and to add connections based on your email contacts from other sites such as Gmail, Hotmail, Yahoo, etc. (there are paid subscriptions that will give you some perks like allowing you to send messages to users that are not in your network, but these subscriptions are not mandatory so it is your choice to decide if you want these or not).

You can build your personal profile by adding your career history, education, skills, specialities, certifications, achievements, websites, a photo and recommendations. By adding a photo you can personalize your profile even more and show everyone how you do not look completely hideous or how pleasant it might be to look at your ugly face for 8 hours a day. We are of course assuming you are not an idiot and you will not upload photos of yourself in a bikini or using a bong onto these websites (unless you are a bikini model or work at a medical marijuana dispensary, then good for you). Remember that social networks are public. You do not want employers to know you are crazy, right? Then do not upload those wacky Ibiza photos from 2006 with you wearing a thong as a hat at a club.

We especially like the recommendations section that allows colleagues and managers to tell everyone how much they did not hate working with you.

How To Ask For A Recommendation

Getting recommendations is tricky. It is all about the best time to ask and how lazy your connections are. You would think that spending 10 minutes writing a short review would be perfectly acceptable for you to ask someone you

17. The Idiot's Guide To Job Hunting

know. But no, you are using up precious time they could be using to fling an angry bird at some pigs or from their Facebook lurking and stalking.

The best time to ask for a recommendation is actually when someone is leaving a job. They will be filled by this need to have some good feedback from colleagues and they know that if they recommend you, you will recommend them. So this is the best time to click on that "Ask for a recommendation" button. If you are thinking of leaving it is best to ask for a recommendation way before you leave.

If you are creating a new profile that is also a good time to ask for a recommendation since people will assume you are a newbie just building your profile.

How To Recommend Other People

Like everywhere else on the Internet you have unwritten "netiquette" rules you should follow. Recommending someone with a *"Love this guy! He can drink you under the table and is also a cool boss!"* is not ok. Surprised? Then maybe LinkedIn is not the tool for you. Maybe you like your burger flipping job. For everyone else, you can continue reading.

Try to remember these short rules:
1. Be pleasant
2. Be professional
3. Use templates (Google is your friend)
4. Do not write something offensive
5. Give useful input on what that person does best
6. Keep it short and sweet

Remember that if that person dislikes what you wrote, they will not accept it and you will not get a recommendation from them. And you have just acted like an ungrateful loser.

A good recommendation should be short (keep it to less than 6 lines), concise, have an introduction that says you are you related to the person, where you met, where you work together, what was their best asset and skill (for example, if they were your favorite manager because they also brought you donuts) and should finish with a nice ending sentence wishing them luck in the future and stating if you would like to work with them again. Try to keep the recommendation honest, since it will appear in your profile as well and there is nothing more annoying than a brown nosed suck up saying good things about their manager just because you want a raise.

Other Social/Work Networking Platforms

We have noticed that other professional online networks have popped up on Facebook, but you need to ask yourself: do you really want to connect recruiters to the drunken photos you took last at that last Christmas party? We didn't think so. We are strong believers that you should always keep your personal life out of your professional life.

Remember that your future manager will Google you, so try to keep your personal life private. It is fine that you took up mummification as a hobby but you might want to share this with your new potential colleagues AFTER they have grown fond of you.

18. How To Become A Mortuary Agent

You decided you want to change careers since you finally realized there are thousands of architects trying to apply for that one job. This is not an easy decision. You worked for years and years to get that dream degree, you watched all the episodes of Law & Order and you think you will be a great lawyer. But real life has proven harder than what you had imagined and now you are disappointed with life and want something better.

Did you read our guide on how to rework your curriculum vitae and cover letter? If after a few months of sending hundreds of emails you are growing desperate, we have an even more desperate solution for you. Change careers.

Some (very few) careers still thrive in a crisis. We wouldn't say you are taking advantage of people in a time of need (if that was true we would be telling you you should become a stockbroker), but a few jobs continue to have high demand because not many people want to do them.

Have you thought about the wonderful world of funerary homes? Unfortunately, people have not stopped keeling over. The world population keeps growing, so more people keep dying of course. It's a question of proportions. Embalming and cremation need technicians for it. If you

18. How To Become A Mortuary Agent

have a strong stomach it might be a good business opportunity.

Apparently there are more qualifications related to wanting to be involved in the world of funeral homes other than to "really dig death" (eww.). If you want to be an embalmer for example, in America you actually need to have an Associate of Arts degree. Apparently it's an art form. If you attend a mortuary school you only need one year of training, if you don't, you need two doing an apprenticeship. If you are into dead bodies, but wish they were a bit prettier, you can become a mortuary makeup artist which is also very well paid. You need cosmetology classes at a beauty school and apparently attending Mortuary Science classes help.

They want you to train on living breathing individuals first before you actually work on corpses because corpses are harder. So whenever you are getting your haircut or makeup applied for your wedding just think that person might be annoyed you have blood pumping in your veins because all they wanted is to work on those calm juicy corpses. You probably disgust them as soon as you stand up from your chair.

Many people think carpentry and plumbing are beneath them. If you knew how much money these jobs actually make due to their specificity you would stop judging these professionals and make your kid pay more attention to his wood shop classes. Carpenters and plumbers were considered to have a better job than air traffic controllers in 2012, since their stress level is lower, salary is similar and work schedules are less tiring.

Troikapocalypse

Parole officers have a very stable job too. If you can deal with criminals there's a future right there too. Be aware that this job involves doubtful parts like collecting pee from criminals so they can be tested for drugs. You also need to study either criminal justice or sociology. Do you really want to go to college just so you can carry around other people's pee with you and deal with all the idiots who have gone to jail but are lucky enough to be out on parole?

If you are still in college, psychologists and psychiatrists have seen their business have a steep rise due to a rise in depression and stress-related diseases worldwide. People are searching for medical help more and more and believe they can't solve their problems themselves and need medical guidance (in pill format or just someone to listen to them) in order to survive the urban jungle. You can either try to talk people off the ledge, or be a pill pusher and make people happy enough with those tiny pills that they will never go anywhere near that ledge.

Always remember, a funeral director earns on average more than a primary school teacher. Primary school teachers have really impressive jobs because they are substituting the role of parents while the parents are away at work earning money to pay bills, but they really should earn more taking into account how tiring their job is. We do not like dealing with other people's brats and they do it most of their day, every day. They get happy with a few success stories, they get way too emotionally involved when things do not go well. So yes, in a way we are saying it is easier to handle corpses than kids. The problem with funeral directors is that you spend more time handling

18. How To Become A Mortuary Agent

heartbroken family members than the actual corpse and you are trying to get money out of them at a really complicated time.

Every job has its pros and cons and you just have to weigh what you really can stomach, what you cannot handle and how much do you care about making more money than you are making right now. Or else you will end up even more unhappy than you were before. It is easier than you think.

We can give you one last example of a career change you could undertake but that you will hate yourself and everyone will hate you for it.

Spamming

We will not give you a manual of how to do this since we hate spammers. You will be paid to troll around online and post links to dodgy websites. It can be very well paid, but you need to be on your computer a lot. A lot.

We would rather you picked up extra work shift hours at a fast food joint. It is better to constantly smell of French fries than to pollute our beautiful internet with trash.

We know you need more money but oh well. Don't say we did not warn you.

19. How To Battle Crisis Depression

You might be feeling a little under the weather. Whenever you turn on the TV there's all this talk of the crisis, little children with flies around their heads asking for money. If you have a heart and it is not made out of tin this might start to get to you.

We do not condone moping around the house complaining to everyone that your life is horrible and there is nothing you can do. There is always something that can cheer you up and get you out of your funk. If you are depressed even getting out of bed is hard, much less heading to work and dealing with constant conversations about "downsizing", less vacation time, more taxes. That is why we decided to compile a little list of tips you can use to feel better. If you feel better you might go after that job you always wanted, or take out that cute girl in the accounting department and be non-depressed with her at some bar, or go volunteer at the local animal shelter.

What You Should Do

Travel

Fortunately with the internet you can find cheap travel deals anywhere. There are hundreds of websites willing to offer you inexpensive vacations that can help you unwind.

19. How To Battle Crisis Depression

We only advise this if you can really afford it, coming back from vacation and looking at your empty bank account will only sink you further into that hole of debt and desperation.

Did you previously go to Brazil or Dubai or Japan every year to unwind? And you cannot afford it anymore? How about a nice weekend getaway at a European destination if you are in Europe or exploring more of what your own country has to offer? We bet you do not know your own country all that well.

Before you book with discount travel agents do research them a little bit to make sure they are trustworthy. Always know where your money is going and if other people had good travel experiences working with that company.

You also should visit review sites for hotels and travel destinations to look for reviews on the hotel and if it is worth staying at to ensure you can have a relaxing time while on vacation. Websites like Tripadvisor collect recent experiences from other guests that will warn you about noisy hotels, dirty hotels rooms, bad hotel locations and the like. If you plan ahead a little bit you will increase your chances of having a very relaxing time away from work.

Bargain Hunt

Some people love to bargain hunt and go into thrift shops and vintage shops looking for that special deal. It sounds annoying to most people but it can be quite relaxing and you might be able to find cheap awesome deals for that coffee table you have been wanting to buy for the past three years but couldn't afford to. This is also true online. Subscribe to newsletters of the websites you shop more at and they will let you know when a sale is going on. Amazon sometimes has great deals on DVDs and Blu-Rays and this can save you a lot of money and can get you more entertainment to get your mind out of the Troikapocalypse.

Redecorate

You can redecorate your house to make it feel a bit more like a home. Before you start planning a very expensive home renovation which can be thousands of Euros or more, why not start with tiny details here and there? Paint that dresser over that you hate and change the knobs and give it a whole new look. There are quite a few websites online that can give you good DIY ideas to spruce up your house and make it feel more yours.

Since we are trying to keep you happy, no painting things black everywhere. Try to use light summer colours. Your house must reflect your personality a little bit but it can also influence it. If your bedroom is all painted black with red curtains and statues of gargoyles everywhere that is OK but you might not wake up very cheerfully.

Find Things To Do For Free

There are plenty of things to do in your neighbourhood for free. We have discussed this before in the chapter "Saving Money". You just need to find your local website that will tell you which activities are available. How about going to an art exhibit or for a walk in a park? That free movie

19. How To Battle Crisis Depression

screening? Go to the beach and take something light to eat and enjoy the sunlight and cold sea water.

It has been scientifically proven that when you are exposed to natural sunlight you are absorbing Vitamin D. Not getting enough sunlight can increase your chances of getting cancer about 70%, along with diseases like diabetes, Alzheimer's, psoriasis, infertility, PMS, etc. Scientists are not sure if people feel more depressed because they will get sick without Vitamin D, or if it's due to the decrease in production of cytokines (proteins that cause inflammation).

Anyway, sunlight is good. Grab your sunscreen and even if you hate going to the beach go to a coffee shop with enough sunlight and go synthesize that happiness a little bit.

Exercise

We know, it is a cliché. But scientific study says we are right. So shut up and go look at some numbers. We already mentioned this before in the "Saving Money" chapter but it really is true that exercise is good for you and will make you feel happier. Sex would help too but this is not a self-help book to improve your love life. On that department you are on your own. Maybe you will meet the person of your dreams at the gym or at the park? At least you will get some eye candy.

Go flex those muscles.

What Not To Do

Troikapocalypse

Spend Money That You Do Not Have

Leave that credit card at home. Your bank might love it but you won't when that bill arrives. If you can't afford something, just don't get it unless you really need it. You need food, to pay your bills, a few other essentials. The rest is basically just crap cluttering your life. We're not saying for you to become a hippy and let go of all materialistic values and go live in a commune, but do really figure out what's essential for you and isn't.

Watch The News Obsessively

It is important to be informed about what is going on in the world but there is no need to overdo it and become obsessed with it. Do stay on top of things and know how the laws are changing, what you need to worry about. But do it with moderation. If it is making you upset step away from online newspapers, news channels and colleagues talking about the crisis 24/7 and go to the movies that evening.

You are not deciding the future of your country so there is no need for you to be on top of things every single hour of the day.

Make Stupid Investments

It is very tempting to think that with this crisis new markets and investment opportunities are just around the corner. Of course there are, we are sure there must be a few billionaire deals going on in the stock exchange. But

19. How To Battle Crisis Depression

unless you know what you are doing, this is very risky and you should not gamble your money away.

This is like you heading to the casino a specific day because you think "it's your lucky day". The casino always wins. So do professional stockbrokers compared with someone just playing around and selling and buying shares without any real knowledge of the inner workings of certain companies.

Avoid Pity Parties

It is human nature to complain. We love getting attention and we love having people around us who care and try to help us. But is talking about how awful your life is helping you at all, or is it just bring yourself down and the people around you? Are they better off than you are? They probably are in the same boat as you.

Be thankful for what you have. You probably still have a job, a family that cares about you, your dog who loves you even if you forget to walk him occasionally (if you have a cat treat him like a God, because if you keep forgetting to feed him and pet him daily, he will try to kill you when you are asleep). You still have a roof over your head. You are basically becoming a victim in the story of your own life. Would you not prefer to be the superhero (or heroine) who saves the day and everyone admires for their strength under stress and adversity?

Try to keep a positive attitude and a smile on your face and things might look up for you. If you go to a job interview acting desperate they will think you are stressed and unpredictable. If you sound confident and calm and under control they will be a lot more impressed. Don't go into that room complaining that you need to pay your bills and that you will have to move back into your parents' house and that the bank is threatening to take your car and your apartment. Chin up and show them the truth: they need you more than you need them.

Avoid reaching such a desperate state that you turn to a life of crime or put other people in danger around you. Your integrity is important. Remember, when you reach rock bottom the only way to go is up.

20. A Recipe For Disaster

Welcome to the world of chicken and tuna

So you keep seeing bills pile up and the amount of money at the end of the month being less and less, even food seems expensive, which it never did before. And you've probably noticed you need to cut expenses somewhere. Where can you cut first? No, do not sell your firstborn, which is slightly illegal and immoral. But you can have him; yourself and your entire family spend less on food. How? Why thank you for asking, we will try to teach you.

Caviar and champagne evenings are over. Well, not really. If you can afford champagne and caviar you are, sorry to say, rich (sorry for us, not you, yay for you). So the crisis probably did not hit you that hard. You keep doing what you are doing and we will keep complaining about how rich you are and how jealous everyone is of you. Why did you even buy this book, were you curious on how the little people were doing? They are not doing very well. If you can throw a few jobs their way that would be great, thank you.

For us common folks, the answers lie on things you would have never thought could help.

Food Recycling (eww...)

Most people hate eating leftovers, us included, though Gary is rather fond of 18 hour old curry. Repeating meals is

20. A Recipe For Disaster

so boring, it is so much easier grabbing a meal at McDonald's than carrying a lunch box around for work. And seriously, McDonald's or any other fast food chain is not that expensive. But if you cook a larger amount of cheaper food and freeze it and take it to work you might be able to save a few Euros per day which will amount to 200 or 300 Euros per month. It does not seem like a lot but it will certainly help, especially if the banks keep increasing your mortgage or gas prices keep going up.

We should write a chapter on how public transportation is amazing but we do not really want to because it would be boring so here it is: buses, trains and metros exist and are a lot cheaper than a car, you do the math.

When you are at home, if you know how to cook without burning your house down, cook larger quantities and get some good Tupperware. Freeze the leftovers. When you go to work grab one of those Tupperware's and voilà, an instant, cheap meal to eat at work. We are assuming your workplace treats you decently and has a common area with a microwave. Do a little bag with cutlery, napkins and take a juice box with you and your meal will also be a lot healthier than eating fast food every day for lunch. Anyone who does this regularly can also tell you a few dishes are much better if they rest after a while, like chili or curry. They actually gain flavour.

Please do not try to freeze salads and the like, those are a whole different ballgame. If you want to take salads to work throw everything into a Tupperware before leaving the house and take the lettuce separately or any other ingredients that when in contact with other soggier ingredients look terrible after a couple of hours.

In Portugal there is a sophisticated name for leftovers which we use to make them sound more posh. We call them redom ("restos de ontem", literally means the remains of yesterday), you pronounce it "raydom". We hope this term catches on internationally, and because we think we are oh so clever, we are renaming it and your Hello Kitty lunch boxes will now include "**redones**" (patent pending). Because they were done again. Get it?

Meat Is Delicious Murder

Meat is expensive. We all know that right? Beef can really hurt your budget at the end of the month. There are cheaper alternatives. Chicken is always pretty inexpensive, and you know you can always rely on that chicken of the sea, the tuna. Certain recipes like lasagne and spaghetti Bolognese can be made replacing the meat with soy meat, which is basically what experts call "textured vegetable protein". Lots of these recipes can withstand freezing. We are not saying you should turn vegetarian but you can vary and make your dishes less expensive to cook at home.

There are plenty of cheap protein alternatives you can cook as well. Those frozen cordon bleus, or chicken patties, or even hamburger meat or veggie burgers. Make something to accompany these like mashed potatoes or a pasta and you're ready to go.

Share Meals

20. A Recipe For Disaster

A friend of ours told us a story recently that sounds like both fun and cheap to imitate. A group of friends of hers created a game where they meet up every week, and one from the group cooks a meal. They do theme nights and go all out with the decoration, the table setting, the music. They do inexpensive meals (who does not love Mexican Night or Thai Night) and they write little evaluation cards at the end of the meal. After the entire group has cooked for one evening they will gather up all the cards and evaluate who is the best chef. It is like a homemade version of television shows like Top Chef or Iron Chef, urging people to cook more at home and eat out less.

Of course we are not saying you should never eat out, restaurants need to survive too, but choose when you go out to dinner more wisely. Paying the bills comes first, having an amazing meal at a restaurant comes second. Unless you enjoy the concept of being homeless-chic, living in your car but having oysters every week. Hey, it's your life, who are we to judge?

We know what you are thinking, so much babbling, where are our money-saving recipes?

These are budget recipes and they are aimed mainly towards things you can freeze easily or keep in the fridge and take to work. So, yes working class, this is all for you. Go buy your Scooby Doo lunch box and get ready for some decent food.

Cheese And Ham Quiche

A very simple quiche you can cook the day before and will give you probably 6 servings. You can eat it either cold or hot. I probably would not try to freeze it cause the puff pastry would get very weird, but hey, you do whatever you want.

You can make variations of this quiche and replace the ham with vegetables like zucchini and broccoli, put in corn, chicken, mushrooms, whatever you want basically.

Ingredients:
4 eggs
1 pack (200 ml) of heavy cream
1 puff pastry dough already pie shaped (we could be all snobbish and tell you to make your own dough but who has the time for that, just buy it)
Lots of cheese
Lots of ham
Salt, pepper and oregano

Preparation:
This is so easy you'll be embarrassed you need to follow a recipe, so we'll be quick. Preheat the oven at 200°C (or 380°F). Stretch the pastry dough and put it in a baking dish for pies, using the non stick sheet that comes with the dough underneath. Use a fork and prick the dough a few times so it cooks more easily.

Cut the cheese and ham into little cubes. In a separate bowl whisk four eggs and the heavy cream together and season it with a little salt, a pinch of oregano and as much

20. A Recipe For Disaster

pepper as you want (we love pepper!). Put the cheese and ham on top of the puff pastry and pour the liquid on top. If you have parmesan cheese you can sprinkle it on top so it gives the pie a nice golden color when it bakes.

Put everything in the oven. It should take about 30 minutes to cook everything evenly. When the liquid is solid and the top and the dough have a nice golden colour it means it's done.

When you take it to work take a separate container with some lettuce and tomato and enjoy!

Vegetable Lasagne

We wanted to put here a chili recipe instead but our stupid writers are very proud of their meat chili recipe and do not want to change it to something cheaper made out of soy meat. So you Google a chili recipe for yourself and our secret decades-old chili recipe will stay a very closely guarded secret. Sorry! Here's a lasagne for you.

Ingredients:
Tomato Sauce
Vegetables (zucchini, aubergine, red bell peppers, onions)
Pre-made lasagne sheets
Mushrooms
Olive Oil
Salt and Pepper
Paprika
Butter
Béchamel Sauce (if you can't find it it's made with milk, cornstarch, butter and nutmeg)
Parmesan cheese

Preparation:
In a very large skillet cook your red bell peppers, onions, zucchini and your mushrooms together in a generous amount of olive oil. When it starts to cook put in the tomato sauce. Throw in lots of paprika for flavour. In a separate bowl cut the aubergine into large disks and season it with salt. Cook them in a separate skillet again with lots of olive oil and in very high heat so they can brown outside and cook evenly. When they're soft and ready add them to the other mixture and mix everything together for flavour.

20. A Recipe For Disaster

Grab an oven container and start building your lasagne. Use the butter on the metal container so that the lasagne doesn't stick. Lay down one layer of lasagne sheets. Put the vegetable mixture on top and cover with another layer of lasagne sheets. Put the béchamel sauce on top of the lasagne sheets and then another layer of the vegetables.

Repeat until the oven tray is full up to the top and then cover everything with béchamel sauce evenly. Sprinkle with parmesan cheese on top.

It takes about 40 minutes in the oven at 220°C (800°F). Keep checking with a knife if the lasagne sheets are properly cooked.

Enjoy!

Tuna Pasta

If you are on a diet you can just skip this one. Seriously, it's cheap, it tastes good, it is NOT low in calories. Don't come and complain to us that you gained 40 pounds. This recipe is made for you to have enough energy to farm fields from dusk until dawn and do some heavy physical labour.

Also, it sounds bizarre, but it's actually quite delicious. Bear with us. It's not haute cuisine but you can make it in 15 minutes.

Ingredients:
Pasta (like spaghetti)
Heavy Cream
Two small tuna cans

Preparation:
This is incredibly easy. Cook the pasta. Put the heavy cream in a skillet and let it heat up. Add the two small cans of tuna to it, after you drain off the oil from the cans. Mix the tuna into the cream until it makes a fairly consistent sauce. Drain the pasta, put it in a dish and put some of the sauce on top.

Stop looking at it weirdly and enjoy it.

20. A Recipe For Disaster

Chicken Stroganoff

A very simple recipe that you can freeze and reheat the next day. Even the rice can take being blasted in the microwave pretty well since the Stroganoff hides the slight change in texture from the reheating.

Ingredients:
Three chicken breasts
Cream
Worcestershire Sauce
Salt and Pepper
Onion
Mushrooms
Basmati Rice

Preparation:
Cut the onions into little cubes. Throw them in a skillet with olive oil and the chopped mushrooms and cook them well. When the mushrooms and the onions are soft, add the three chicken breasts chopped into thin strips.

While you are doing this get some water boiling in a pot with salt and start your rice (if you are new at this cooking thing, this is how you make rice, boiling water! Impressive isn't it?).

Cook the chicken in the same pan (previously seasoned with salt and pepper, we love our pepper, remember this) until it is very well done since nobody likes uncooked chicken. When the chicken is starting to look cooked through (no rosy bits) add two tablespoons of Worcestershire sauce to the mix.

Five minutes of cooking should cook the sauce enough to remove the acidic taste from the Worcestershire Sauce. In the end add the cream and mix it very well.

20. A Recipe For Disaster

Summer MAN Salad

We know you guys are immediately thinking "I'm not eating a damn salad, I need my meat!". Calm down. This is a MAN salad. It will have enough ingredients to feed your testosterone. Remember, lettuce goes in just before you are going to eat it. Do not freeze the lettuce... we warned you.

Ingredients:
Fusilli pasta (want to be healthier? Whole grain pasta)
Canned peaches
Lettuce
Walnuts
Your favourite cheese
Turkey Ham
Corn
Caesar Salad Sauce (or any other sauce, just use your favourite sauce, like mayo. Buy it or make it at home)
Avocado

Preparation:
Boil the pasta. Cut everything into a bowl except for the lettuce. When you are ready to serve it put the lettuce on the plate. Pour your chosen sauce over it. Not that hard, was it?

Szechwan Eggplant Stir Fry

Ingredients:
3 big eggplants
Olive oil
Salt and black pepper
One big onion (use 2 green onions if you can find them)
3 garlic cloves, minced
1 fresh red chilli, sliced (or red chili flakes)
1/2 cup chicken broth
3 tablespoons soy sauce
1 tablespoon rice vinegar
1 tablespoon light brown sugar
1 tablespoon cornstarch

Preparation:
Cut the eggplants lengthwise and then into thin slices so they are easier to cook in a skillet.

Heat a pan (if you are really a dork in the kitchen, a wok) and add the olive oil. Add a layer of eggplant, stir-fry until it's cooked through and soft. Season with salt and pepper. Remove and make another batch of eggplant. Add olive oil whenever needed.
After all the eggplant is cooked through, add the onions, the garlic and chilli. Stir fry for a minute. Add the broth afterwards. In a separate bowl mix the soy sauce, sugar, cornstarch and vinegar together until the sugar has disappeared into the mix. Pour it into the mix and let it thicken for a minute. Add the eggplant back and wait until the sauce is absorbed.

You can serve this Stir Fry with white rice. It is delicious

20. A Recipe For Disaster

and easy to heat after being frozen. There you go, now you know how to make Chinese food, aren't you proud of yourself?

Enjoy!

P.S. Who knew eggs grew on plants? – Gary.

21. What If Civilisation Were To Collapse?

We do believe that while you think an economic crisis is the worst thing that could happen, there are far far worse things out there just waiting for us to be distracted by our petty first world problems. So we'll stop moaning about the Euro and we will give you a few horrible scenarios that will make you get up tomorrow and appreciate that the sun is shining and the skin is not melting off your face. We had many to choose from but we narrowed it down to three awesome catastrophic ones.

Post Apocalyptic Wasteland

So, the worst possible outcome has come to pass. Civilization has collapsed, civil unrest quickly gives way to anarchy. Mankind, or at least sections of it, descends into what can only be described as savagery. What used to be entertaining when you watched the Mad Max films is now your daily life, and doesn't entertain quite so much anymore. The rule of law is gone and you need to protect yourself. So how do you do that?

There are many ways, but working on the assumption that there is always someone with a bigger weapon than you, we are left with only one sensible solution.

You need to build a thermonuclear device.

21. What If Civilisation Were To Collapse?

Quite why the Iranians are (according to the Americans and Israelis) having so much trouble with this is beyond us, it is not all that hard.

Depending on if you want to get the materials ready before civilisation collapses, or try to acquire them after, is up to you. You might have some trouble getting mail order deliveries in the End Times though.

First, you will need some uranium. This step will be easiest if you live in America. Take for example the Kerr-McGee plant near Crescent, Oklahoma. It is best remembered as being where Karen Gay Silkwood worked at the time of her suspicious death. In addition to having a fantastic name, she made plutonium fuel pellets for nuclear reactors.

Believing there were seriously bad things going on at the nuclear fuel plant, she contacted a New York Times journalist and made arrangements to meet and hand over documents to prove her claims. She was last seen in a café, on her way to this meeting, with a binder full of documents. Soon after she was dead, in highly suspicious circumstances, and the documents had vanished.

This is a plant that on two separate occasions "lost" sizeable amounts of plutonium. The plutonium was listed as found, though there has never been any actual proof that this is the case. A Kerr-McGee supervisor, when asked about security measures, stated that "there were none of any kind, no guards, no fences, no nothing." Stealing from them apparently isn't very hard.

If you want to make it even easier, a good target would be the General Atomics fuel fabrication plant in San Diego. Full plans for this facility are available to anyone at the Nuclear Regulatory Commission's reading room at 1717 H Street NW Washington D.C. 20555. A photocopier is available for use.

If that proves to be too difficult, find a university with a TRIGA Mark II reactor. These are helpfully filled with uranium that is around 20% U-235. You would need to enrich it to around 90% U-235 for bombs.
Security in universities is normally less than that at fuel fabrication plants. $50 or so will no doubt buy you a couple of drunk frat boys to create a diversion.

The other option would be to simply buy it. Now you are probably thinking, "don't be stupid, you can't just buy uranium". Not true. For Commercial grade, about 20% U-235, it will set you back about $50 per pound. You will need around 10 lbs of U-235 to make a bomb, so you'll need a fair bit more of the un-enriched stuff.

Your uranium will arrive as uranium oxide. A brownish powder, not too different from instant coffee. Safety tip : do not attempt to make coffee with the uranium! First step will be to convert this into a liquid. Unlike coffee, hot water will not cut it here. You are going to need a few gallons of concentrated hydrofluoric acid. Also plastic containers to keep it in, since it will eat through pretty much everything else.

Mix the uranium with the acid, and you will have yourself a

21. What If Civilisation Were To Collapse?

batch of liquid uranium tetrafluoride. Next, you need to bubble some fluorine gas (again, available from any decent chemical supply depot) through it to create uranium hexafluoride. Safety tip : Fluorine gas is way more lethal than chlorine gas, used as a chemical weapon in World War I. Handling it might be extremely dangerous.

Now comes enrichment. Whack the uranium hexafluoride in a bucket, attach a rope, and swing round your head as fast as you can for around 45 minutes. Since U-235 is lighter, it should have formed a film on top, scoop it up like cream. Repeat until you have enough of the U-235.

To turn it back into a metal, dump a load of calcium in there, any decent pharmacist can sell you this. You'll get uranium metal, and calcium fluoride, a colourless salt, easy to separate. once you have the uranium, you will need 2 metal bowls, as close to perfect hemispheres as possible. half the uranium goes in each.

That last part is particularly important, don't keep it all together! Criticality accident is not a good way to go. Sure, it looked cool on Stargate, with it ending with Daniel Jackson evolving into a "higher being", but that is fairly unlikely to happen to you.

Ideally, your bowls should be of a size that means they can fit inside a cylindrical vacuum cleaner. Uranium is a soft metal like gold, so grab a hammer, and bang away at it till it is shaped into 2 hemispheres inside the bowls.

Now we need a way to bring these together with a fair bit of force. So we need explosives. Gunpowder is fairly easily made at home from potassium nitrate, sulphur and carbon. Even better would be some TNT or blasting caps which can be purchased from construction sites.

Best of all would be some C4 plastic explosives. If we are living in a Mad Max style apocalypse, raiding any nearby military depots should have been the first thing you did after they were abandoned. you can shape the C4 like plasticine around the bowls, giving a nice even explosion.

Next, take your bowls and secure into opposite ends of the vacuum cleaner. Use masking tape to hold them in place. if you have moulded C4 to them add detonators and you are almost done. if you've gone for a lower tech solution, add your explosives in a way that when it blows, it will force the two halves toward each other. for now you want to keep them at least a foot (30cm for our European readers) apart. This helps to prevent horrifying, premature death.

You now have a fairly simple atomic bomb. likely to cause a fair amount of damage, but given the size, it would be a small tactical device, a bit smaller than the devices that were detonated in Hiroshima and Nagasaki. There are a few ways to punch up the power.

Rather than centrifuging your uranium by hand, you could use a commercial centrifuge.

You might also want to be more fussy in the design and building stage. For example when the explosives go off to bring the two half's of your critical mass together, the ideal situation is it goes off all around at the same time, and exerts the same force on all points of the surface at the

21. What If Civilisation Were To Collapse?

same time. C4 is best for that. the more evenly it is spread over the surface of the bowls, the better.

Finally, you may want to upgrade to a hydrogen bomb. increasing the power of the resulting explosion by several orders of magnitude.

For this you will need another 3 of the bombs you just built, as close to identical as you can make them. You'll also need around 100 pounds of lithium deuteride, costing around $1000 per pound from any chemical supply company. Alternatively you could use lithium hydride at $40 per pound.

Place all this in glass containers and position between the 4 fission bombs you have built. Setting them all off simultaneously would produce a fusion explosion able to level a city.

If you are able to convince enough people that you would happily blow yourself up along with anyone foolish enough to attack you, your nuclear deterrent should help you create your own new nation.

Or maybe see you vaporised when the whole crazy scheme goes wrong.

Natural Disasters

In case you did not know, we have a few dormant volcanoes that could cause massive devastation to entire continents. One of these lies beneath Yellowstone National Park in the United States of America. If it blew it would be at least a thousand times stronger than Mount St. Helens. It is called a caldera since it doesn't have a mountain on top of it, it is basically a big hole of despair waiting to spit out Hell and Fire on us when we least expect it. Predictions are that if it became active it would create an ash cloud that would cover America and would get into the jet stream rendering transatlantic flights impossible, while ruining most of the world's food production at the same time. Why? Because it is evil and wants us to both choke and starve at the same time. Hundreds of thousands of people would die in a matter of days.

Like Yellowstone there is also a super volcano in Iceland and another in Hawaii. You would think one would be enough to frighten us. Next time you think about taking a nice relaxing vacation to Hawaii you might want to think twice if you want to sunbathe on top of the Mouth of Hell.

If any of these decide to show us how powerful they are within our lifetimes one thing is guaranteed, we can stop worrying about the economic crisis and can start worrying about basic survival.

We were going to create a whole other category dedicated to the possibility of an asteroid hitting the Earth but we don't want to bore you with natural disasters. So yes, another possibility is a big chunk of stone being hurled towards our planet by the vengeful Universe who really doesn't like us going on expeditions out there and leaving out all kinds of trash (tens of millions of pieces! We Humans should really not be allowed to go anywhere; we don't know how to pick up after ourselves).

21. What If Civilisation Were To Collapse?

The probability of an asteroid hitting the Earth has been measured by scientists and they say the odds are a million to one against it happening in the next one hundred years. You can sleep peacefully without worrying it's going to wipe out Civilization. For now.

We will use this opportunity to warn future generations that if the oceans ever reach a temperature of over 50°C, something bad may come our way. A hypercane. Yes, that word exists. It is a hurricane that is so big and massive it could engulf an entire continent. A hyper hurricane. It could have winds that reach 800km/h (500 mph/h). Can you imagine the force on that beast? You of course cannot, and if you ever encountered one you would not either, because you would be very dead.

Why would an ocean be that hot? Global warming, that damn asteroid again, or our friends the super volcanos.

Are you scared of natural disasters now? After recent events, with the 2004 Indian Ocean Tsunami, the Haiti Earthquake, Katrina and the Japanese Earthquake of 2011, we can conclude natural disasters are not that uncommon. We just hope none of us get to see one these destructive forces up close. We would rather deal with the zombies. Yes, zombies.

Brain Eating Zombies

New diseases pop up every single day around the world. Viruses mutate at an alarming rate and scientists have a hard time keeping up. Even the virus for the common cold

Troikapocalypse

mutates at such a rapid rate that new vaccines come out on a yearly basis.

We however do not believe a virus could turn a human into a walking brain-eating corpse.

Apparently a person does not need to be dead to crave human meat. There have been cases in the news of people, either under the influence of drugs, or just plain crazy, attempting to eat human flesh. Random attacks have been reported. So we can very scientifically conclude that zombies are real, are out there now, and are terrifying.

You should prepare for the inevitable zombie apocalypse. Everything from basic supplies to an underground bunker would be useful. If you become convinced the zombie apocalypse has indeed begun, those of you who are brave and/or foolish enough should begin eradication efforts immediately. You should be fully certain that you are not being premature in declaring the zombie apocalypse underway.

While eradication efforts should be undertaken with gusto, if it turns out you have killed half your neighbours and they were only suffering from a severe bout of the flu, and not in fact some form of zombieism, you are likely to do a fair amount of jail time. A premature apocalypse declaration is fairly unlikely to be of any use as a defence.

Make sure they try to eat your brain before you get out your shotgun.

22. Ideas For Supplemental Income

Everyone loves having extra money. Unless you are one of those bizarre people who likes just living off love and charity, most people enjoy being independent, paying their bills and still have money to go out and party with their friends. Sometimes money doesn't last until the end of the month though. There are two ways you can go about it. You can either try to save where you can, and we have already taught you all about it, or you can figure out how to get some extra Euros (or pounds, dollars, etc.). And we will assume you gave up on the idea of becoming a criminal mastermind since most of us can't do the evil laugh anyway (the "muahahahah" is not easy).

Crowd funding

First and foremost, and we have to mention this, there is crowd funding. We do not support creating a "help me go on vacation" project because those are incredibly annoying, and there are so many crowd funding projects out there it will just get lost in all the garbage online. Do you have a fun creative new idea, a project or product you would love to start working on but don't have your own money to inject into it? That's what websites like Indiegogo and Kickstarter are for. You need to captivate your audience with something new and exciting that they really want to have. Or if you want just create a charitable project

22. Ideas For Supplemental Income

("save the endangered sea monkeys") that won't get you extra money but is close to your heart and will make you sleep better at night.

If you have a pet project like making cute bracelets with real stardust or a new iPhone accessory that you always wanted (somebody is already making a taser that is also a phone cover, how cool is that?) this is the way to get the project off the ground without injecting money you don't have.

Be prepared to invest a lot of time and effort into your new brilliant idea though, crowd funding implies pissing a lot of people off by being extremely annoying and selling your idea. You will have to email, talk about the project, use social networking websites and do all the footwork yourself.

Getting An Extra Job

A second job is a really good idea if you have the time off to do it. Killing yourself with work might not be a good idea if you already work eight hours a day. Some things like sleep and socializing and eating were not invented just to fill up your time. But if you don't work that many hours and think you can use that free time, maybe looking for a second part-time job is the solution for you. If you work in a very specific area like IT and you know short consulting jobs are available over the weekends or it is something you can do during the evenings instead of spending your night at the pub spending the money you don't have, go for it.

If you do want to open an independent business supplying

this new service you need to declare it to the big bad government and they will want your tax money. So do the math and figure out if it'll be worth it at the end of the year when you hand in your taxes and what expenses and income you need to declare. Sometimes this extra cash flow sounds exciting until you find out you are injecting more money than you are making.

Selling Your Body

Whoa, get your mind out of the gutter. Prostitution is illegal almost everywhere in the world. If you are going down that path you are a lot worse than we initially thought and our book might not save you.

Selling your organs on the black market is also very illegal and extremely dangerous so we do not condone or support it. A Chinese teenager recently sold his kidney (and subsequently suffered renal failure) to buy a new iPhone and iPad. Even if his stupid plan had gone well imagine how dumb he must feel whenever a new generation of Apple products comes out. Nine people are on trial for helping and benefiting from this completely idiotic idea. Let's hope he gets a kidney AND a brain transplant.

Some countries pay people to participate in clinical trials for new drugs. While this also sounds stupid, in some very rare cases it might not be the worst idea ever. If you suffer from blinding migraines for example, and no medication works for you, a clinical trial may help you, and you would be helping other people in the long run. You just have to weigh in the pros and cons carefully. Maybe go to a clinical trial for something actually wrong with you and realize you

22. Ideas For Supplemental Income

might turn orange, or have a lot of flatulence, or something even worse. You might get the placebo (there is always a control group) but the human brain is a wonderful thing and you will probably suffer some side effects anyway because your brain will be conditioned to believe you should be growing a third nipple.

Sperm Whale

If you are a man endowed with a penis, you might have your money maker right there in your pants. Some clinics will pay for sperm donations to help couples who can't have children. This is also true for women and their unfertilized eggs.

Since we hate dumb people and believe our readers are extremely intelligent, we are in favour of you donating your high IQ genes to other people. Making the next generation smarter is a very noble cause!

We hope you are not intimidated by masturbating into a cup. Just use your imagination and think that in twenty years you might be walking down the street and you could bump into a teenager that looks eerily like you.

Inheriting

You do know most people are born into money instead of earning it through blood, sweat and tears, right? You can work your entire life and still make less than what Paris Hilton spends on a purse or a pair of shoes.

Maybe the good tip here is, actually get along and like your family. Instead of resenting that rich secluded uncle who never sent you a Christmas postcard, get to know him. When he croaks your name might actually show up in his will. You might get an old worthless vase or you might get an insane amount of money, who knows, but it never hurts to actually be nice.

This works the other way around too since you should "be nice to your children, they will choose your nursing home". So if you don't want to share a room with three senile old ladies and never have any visitors, appreciate your children as the ones who will save you from a humiliating end.

It sounds cynical, but it is good advice. Be nice to everyone!

Create A Cult

If you are a despicable human being who likes to explore other people's weaknesses you might turn to the religious route and create your own cult following. People like giving money to religious leaders who they think will be their saviours.

If you do look at famous cult leaders most of them started off with nothing and ended up with an empire. We of course have to mention L. Ron Hubbard and his "Church of Scientology". After being a moderately successful science-fiction and fantasy writer he decided he needed to create a Church based on his ideas on Dianetics, where we are all immortal beings who have forgotten our true meaning on this Earth. L. Ron Hubbard went from being a

22. Ideas For Supplemental Income

normal middle class citizen to owning houses, apartments, land, boats, everywhere in the world. His Sea Organization owns one of the biggest yachts in the world.

Stewart Traill created the Forever Family, now known as the Church of Bible Understanding. He might have started as a vacuum repairman but this cult leader now owns several airplanes and his own mansion. His followers donate 90% of their salaries to the church.

Maharishi Yogi, the famous guru leader who gave the Beatles their mantras, is suspected to be immensely rich despite almost everyone thinking he faded into obscurity. He is estimated to be worth billions of dollars, even more than Reverend Moon, the leader of the Unification Church and David Miscavige himself, the current leader of Scientology. These people basically own their own empires.

Several pastors in Nigeria are worth more than one million dollars, so this not only happens in cults, even supposedly trustworthy Christian leaders take advantage of their followers. It's not hard to find photos of Bishop David Oyedepo enjoying his private jet online. His net worth is $150 million.

We are not saying you should do it, but it does kind of work. So go out there, make yourself a fancy tinfoil hat, pick an amusing name for your religion (something that sounds fairly serious) and go preach to a street corner. Maybe someone will hear you and will join you in your crazy ways.

Troikapocalypse

Here are very important instructions on how to make your own tinfoil hat:
1. Go to your mother's kitchen
2. Find tinfoil
3. Steal it
4. Cut a large sheet (big enough for your head)
5. Wrap around top of head
6. Twist the top until it looks like an antenna. This will be important to receive signals from aliens
7. If it feels flimsy, add extra tinfoil. You can never use enough tinfoil
8. If you have colourful stickers get them on there. "Jesus is behind the wheel" would be appropriate

You are now ready to go out and make yourself heard. Or get arrested. Do not try to do this naked unless you want to be the guy on the news, naked, in a tinfoil hat. No one talks to that guy, except to mock him.

If you do try to conquer the world through the evil ways of exploiting people's beliefs and weaknesses, we hope you don't mind being hated for being a sociopath and a parasite of society. Religion is the opiate of the people and you will probably find someone to follow you. If Heaven and Hell really do exist though expect a visit downstairs when you die. You kind of deserve it.

23. Procrastination

We have left this chapter till the end. It seemed appropriate...

Everyone has the potential to be a master procrastinator. This book would most likely never have gone beyond the planning stages if not for the actions of a vicious taskmaster who we will not name (*cough*Rita*cough*). Having said that, her cracking of the whip has no doubt been the driving force that has brought this book from an idea, to an actual finished product. We would also be remiss here if we did not mention that the first draft of this chapter contained a fantastic typo which claimed the whipping of the crack was the reason we were motivated. There was, as you can imagine, much laughter!

Procrastination, it turns out, is not always a bad thing. Everyone does it at points. Often the level of socially acceptable procrastination is wildly different depending on the local culture. How much of this perception is fair, and how much is an unfair stereotype, is open to debate.

Professor Jin Nam Choi of the Seoul National University is as associate professor of "Organizational Behaviour and Human Resource Management" and has a PhD in Organisational Psychology from the University of Michigan. He has spent a fair amount of time studying procrastination. This, we believe, is absolute genius. You see, when you are studying procrastination, it essentially

23. Procrastination

gives you license to procrastinate, and yet refer to it as legitimate research. If you are going to pass yourself off as an expert on something, then you need to have experience of the subject.

Professor Choi has determined that there are two kinds of procrastinators: Active and Passive. The passive variety, he claims, postpone making decisions until the last minute due to an actual inability to make decisions in a timely manner. The active variety, he believes, are driven by a belief, consciously or otherwise, that they will do better when they are in a situation where last minute decisions are necessary.

Let's focus on the Active procrastinators. Unlike the passive kind, actives are useful and productive members of society, though to be fair they probably raise the stress levels of everyone around them who would not be classed as an active procrastinator. You see, we don't think we delay on account of being incompetent or incapable of decision making. We believe it's more likely we are busy with other stuff, and have prioritised the important bits. It is also possible we are full of it and are just being lazy!

Many see procrastination as an undesirable trait, something that is not a good indicator of a person's character. Procrastination is an art form. Like any other art form, it can be done well, or badly. If you can do it well, it's likely to help you organise your life to suit you, and not the whims of others.

Postponing... At Work

Some may think that leaving things at work to the last minute is a bad idea. These people are wrong. Procrastination allows you to both prioritise your own time, and appear as a miracle worker in the eyes of your colleagues. There is a lesson to be learned from Star Trek here. You see Scotty had a system where he would estimate repairs as taking four times as long as the time he knew he could do them in, thus creating the illusion that he was able to perform miracles.

Always know when something is needed. Then, when someone asks just before that deadline if you have it, you say no, and ask when it is needed for. Whatever the response, look worried, claim that it is going to take way longer than that, but you will get right on it and see what you can do. Assuming you have not let the procrastination get out of hand, you will be able to finish it in the allotted time, and do it well. If you pull this trick with perfect timing, when it is something that matters, you will quickly gain a reputation as someone who comes through when it is needed. The fact this impression is not really deserved is unimportant. Please use this sparingly and wisely before you are classified as the idiot who never knows any deadlines and has no idea of what is going on around him.

The unfortunate truth is that appearances are often more important than reality in business. Having a few influential people remember you as the guy who came through on short notice that one time is often far better for your career than five years of excellent work that was completed with plenty of time to spare.

23. Procrastination

Another area where procrastination can be your friend is when dealing with emails. There is a school of thought that suggests that replying to any and all emails you receive, as soon as possible after receiving them, shows you are engaged with your job and your colleagues. The proponents of this theory are dullards with no imagination, though if they have the ability to fire you, it is probably best if you do not inform them of this fact.

Email can be a useful tool, but it can quickly degenerate into a load of nonsense chatting. Now we are not against nonsense chatting, but this is typically the time when people will slip in requests for information or for you to do something for them. Being nice people (stop laughing!), we often give the information, or perform the little favour. The problem though, is that at least some of these people have used you as the first port of call, even before expending the smallest amount of effort to find the solution themselves. Leaving it just that little bit longer before responding might mean they have figured the answer machine is not paying out today and they should do something drastic like use Google.

Do not feed the terminally lazy. They will coast by on your assistance and from time to time even appear to be hardworking productive members of the team, mostly on the back of your kindness. This is procrastination combined with sneakiness, a most unacceptable combination as they get by on the skills of others, and not their own.

Another common trait of this type of person is being

completely in love with the idea of organizing "meetings". You know the type. You are dragged to a conference table somewhere, and are subjected to an effect that slows time to a crawl with an efficiency normally reserved for the time dilation effects of a black hole. There are people who believe this is an effective use of time, sitting around a table for hours discussing abstract concepts and goals. Due to the fact that more would be achieved by attempting to explain nuclear physics to a bunch of goats, these people are in error. Have your laptop with you. Spend the time doing something useful while occasionally nodding and muttering "sounds good".

You want to be known as the person who can work the miracles. The person who is always able to step in and take something over, who can board the sinking ship and make it float. Do this without seeming like you spend half of your time on the useless minutia. People always say you should work hard. We prefer to think you should work smart.

Postponing... At Home

Leaving the office behind, we move on to all that snail mail that drops through your door that cannot be classified as junk. There are differing ways to deal with this. We have a wide range of approaches. At one end of the scale, there is the careful checking of it all followed by taking any actions indicated by the checking, then a careful sorting and storing of any documents that could possibly be needed in future. Usually after having hidden them in a drawer until getting one more piece of paper inside would require a violation of the laws of physics.

23. Procrastination

At the other end of the scale it is a fair bit simpler. Open the envelopes as they arrive and ascertain if a response is needed soon to avoid undesirable consequences. If so, do what needs done, if not, well, it should go straight to the shredder.

Whichever method you prefer, try to stick to it. The internet, TV and whatever games system you favour are all very tempting distractions. The chances are that your specific interests will provide at least a couple of other potential diversions. Try and set up a system where you only do the things you like after you have dealt with some of the more boring tasks that come with having your own place. Fridge needs cleaning? Do it, but spend the next 4 hours lounging around enjoying yourself.

We people like to think of ourselves as the pinnacle of evolution. Unfortunately the same tricks that can be used to make the small excitable dog sit still for a few minutes are also effective in having us live up to our responsibilities. Rewards for doing stuff we would rather not do is as effective for us as it is for any other animal.

Paperwork, who needs it. One of our writers piles it up in a secret drawer until it reaches a point where it needs to be sorted. And then an entire day is needed to sort it because you will want to do every single thing at home before sorting out those bank statements. So yes, procrastinating at home is an even bigger art form because you have two wonderful things at home: television and internet.

Learn a balance and set goals and rewards. Change that

light bulb, time for ice-cream. One hour of cleaning out the fridge might earn you an hour of television. It seems childish but we are all children after all and punishment/reward is still an extremely effective method.

If you really want to avoid doing something maybe you can do other tasks around the house that are not as important but will make you feel marginally productive?

What About Life Decisions?

There are some decisions which can have a significant impact on your life. Changing or quitting your job, buying a new car or house, even moving to abroad to a new country. All of these things deserve at very least a few days of consideration before you decide.

Have you decided that you just have to have that new car? Has your old one barely lost the new car smell? Stop and think of the where your finances will be in a couple of years if you keep your old as opposed to where they would be with the new one. If the new car is cheaper, and you'd actually be better off, there may be some wisdom in it. The comparative engine size or if it's a hybrid also should be taken into account, if you'll save a load on fuel it makes the change a fairly attractive one.

Even when the item is question is not expensive enough to have a major impact on your life, you should still take some time to see if you really need it. We all love the new Macbook Pro (except Gary, who believes Mac owners are alien scouts, here ahead of the main invasion), but if you

23. Procrastination

bought one last year, the chances are it has a few years at very least before you actually need a new one.

Just remember there is a difference between useful procrastination and being lazy. Weighing your options when thinking of quitting your job is sensible, but when you've been doing it for 5 years while stuck in the same dead end job, well you are just deluding yourself.

Get Some Sleep

New studies have shown that you might even be doing some work while you are sleeping. According to Maarten Bos, an academic who researches decision making and the unconscious mind at Harvard Business School, we use our brain the whole time. Sleep is associated with better memory performance and it apparently increases our ability to make mental connections and integrate unassociated information. So it is like owning a computer you always run at 20% its capacity but while it is on sleep mode it is running at 95% and processing all the information you gathered that day, week or life.

This is amazing for discovering creative solutions to problems you have been stuck with and can potentially help you make tough decisions. We know people who work in IT and do programming and keep notepads near their bed for when they dream about a solution they had not thought about before. Inventors are known for doing the same thing. Why? The unconscious mind knows how to prioritise important information and ignore the trivial.

So taking an extra night to make an important decision or

give extra thought to a problem at work or in your personal life might actually be helpful. You are not being lazy, you are taking your time and using your super brain.

Do Less, Not More

Recent studies have shown that 60-hour work weeks actually result in a 25% decrease in productivity. People spend so much time at work being unhappy and doing extra work at home and from their smart phones and on vacation that they are saturated and tend to slack more as a way to "rebel" against the system. That and stealing stationery. Confess, how many permanent markers and pens do you have at home from your office? We thought so.

You need to learn how to say no to way too much work. When you are overwhelmed you will be less productive and the work you actually produce will have less quality than it should have.

Learn how to prioritize and get the big important tasks done first, the ones that will land you in unemployment faster. If after six hours you have accomplished those nobody really cares if you forgot to email the pictures for the office party happening in a few months. We all have a tendency to say yes to everything people ask of us at work but that only results in having to choose what actually gets done or what is dropped. A few people try to frantically multitask but we are back to what we said before, quality suffers.

Sometimes less is indeed more, so stop accepting

23. Procrastination

everything they throw at you and just do what you have to do, but better.

An Art Form

The art of procrastination can be useful in many ways. Mastering the art can have benefits in all areas of your life. If done correctly, it can lead to improvements in both your personal and professional lives, as well as giving you more control over your life. You can fit in your relaxing times, often when you want, as opposed to on the schedule of others. And you also get the kick-start of needing to get into gear and do stuff now (though normally not unexpectedly) when deadlines come around.

The beauty is in the balance.

24. To Conclude...

This book started off as a simple conversation between friends. Could we really write a book on a subject we were not experts in? We had no idea but we figured there was really only one way to find out. While it wasn't easy, we had a load of fun doing it. As you've probably figured out by now, we don't think life should be taken all that seriously!

One thing we hope you take from this book is that you are the only one who can make things happen for you. If you are not happy with your life, change it. Always moaning about your job? Well unless you are actively trying to find a new one, stop it, you are just wallowing in pity. Get off your arse and do something. We have just proven anyone can write a book. Find something you want to do, and go do it.

Have you been dreaming about volunteer work in South America for years? Well why haven't you done something about it? You will probably end up with Dengue fever, but no pain no gain. Maybe you're closer to middle age than you want to admit. Do you have the sneaking suspicion that if you could do it all again, you would do some of it differently? Well you can. Go back to college, learn new things, take control.

You shouldn't be afraid of change. We are not telling you to jump into the abyss and become a circus performer. You

24. To Conclude...

can look for a new job while you are still working your previous one. You can work and study at the same time. You can join a gym and go make yourself feel better in your free time, not to mention the health benefits beyond the effect on your mood.

You can always invite your friends around more for dinner or drinks. Start there.

Wow, we'll shut up about that before we start sounding like a "yes you can" self-help book.

If you have found that you have been helped by the reading of this magnificent book, well we feel that you should reward us. We accept Gold, Dollars and British pounds. No Euros please! Well unless you double the reward of course. We will also accept property, as long as it's not in need of repairs. Or a boat, or a plane, or...

Well you get the idea.

Europe will survive. It has endured countless problems, a plague or two, dictators and conquerors, petty fights between neighbours, invasions, earthquakes and Eurovision. For years on end the Europeans have been through good and bad times, and they always survived in style. In the words of the famous Persian proverb, "this too shall pass".

We will always be around, like cockroaches. It doesn't matter what currency Europe will be using and if we are still small nations or one big United States of Europe. This vicious cycle of falling down and getting back up better and stronger will continue.

We survived the Middle Ages; we believe we can survive a fictional crisis about money and power struggles.

Glossary

Angela Merkel - If Europe had a Queen, a ruthless Queen, Angela Merkel would be it. Angela Merkel is the Chancellor of Germany. Since Germany is one of the most powerful countries of the European Union, she is de facto the Leader of the European Union, being on the number one spot of the Forbes' List for Most Powerful Women in the world. Every European Union meeting that is actually important has her present.

Austerity - A very bad word for many in Europe. This is a method of reducing a government's deficit by increasing taxes and/or reducing spending. For government employees this can mean wages being slashed. Also known as the government screwing people over after they have ruined everything. Unemployment rises and you have to assume everyone in power is stupid because they're surprised about this.

Bailout - When it has all gone tits up, bailouts are needed. Normally by giving the destitute more loans, at a lesser interest rate than the market would charge, or by guaranteeing loans so the interest isn't charged at loan shark rates. In the case of banks, a bailout is when they are given loads of money and expected to turn it into more, so they can pay it back. A questionable strategy considering they ended up needing a bailout in the first place.

Balanced Budget - When all the money that is spent by a government is paid for the money it brings in, and as such there is no need to take on additional debt.

Bank Run - When large numbers of people attempt to withdraw all their money at once, possibly in too short a timescale for the bank to be able to pay it all, possibly leading to the collapse of the bank. Telling people that trying to take the money is what could lead to them losing

Glossary

it is normally about as successful as attempting to explain physics to small dogs.

Bankruptcy - A process in which those with big debts are made to sell off everything they own to pay back what they can off their debts. The bright side is that any debts this doesn't manage to pay are written off, which for people means they are debt free and can start again. The exact level to which the bankrupt get screwed by this process depends on which country it is taking place in.

Bond - A debt security. Essentially these are loans. But in what we assume is an attempt to confuse people, they are called bonds. A company or country will sell a bond, meaning they say that they want an amount of money, the market and credit rating will determine the interest rate they need to pay, and they will get the money from whoever buys the bond. The seller in turn makes money from the interest being paid. So yeah. Bond = Loan

Credit Rating - A measure of how safe a debt is from an investment point of view, from AAA to D. These are determined by ratings agencies and play a large part in determining how much interest a borrower pays. This is the process by which countries in trouble are charged incredibly high interest rates, which lead to them getting into a worse situation.

Default - A default has occurred when a borrower fails to repay a loan, not respecting his financial obligations according to the debt contract. This can happen for two reasons, if the lender is unable or unwilling to pay his or her debt.

Deficit - A deficit is a shortfall of revenue, when the amount of money being spent is higher than the amount being earned. If you want to sound really posh, you can say expenditures or liabilities exceed income or assets.

Drachma - The currency used by Greece up until Greece adopted the Euro in 2002. If Greece would abandon the Euro it would mean probably a return to the Drachma so it has been in the news often. Other currencies that could return are the Spanish Peseta and the Portuguese Escudo.

Troikapocalypse

Euro - The currency used by 17 of the 27 member states of the European Union, along with 5 other European countries. It was first adopted and started circulating in 2002. Euros are printed and managed by the European System of Central Banks (ESCB). Its main benefits were removing exchange rates between countries and facilitating trade and the movements of its citizens using the same currency among the many countries that use it. Its problems? Did you even read the other chapters?

Eurozone - The Eurozone, officially the Euro Area, is an economic and monetary union of 17 European Union (EU) member states which have adopted the euro currency as their sole legal tender. Sometimes when talking about the Eurozone people include the other 5 European countries who also use the Euro.

Eurobonds - A Eurobond is an international bond that is denominated in a currency not native to the country where it is issued, so it's also called an external bond. Meaning it's an IOU paper but instead of being national it's international. It is a debt security that secures the indebtedness of the bond issuer to the bearer.

G20 - The finance ministers and central bank governors from 20 major economies, 19 Nations and the European Union. an invite-only group with little power to do anything unless they all agree.

GDP - Gross Domestic Product, the total market values of goods and services produced by a country over a period of time, one of the most widely used economic indicators to see how well nations are doing and so we can compare them to each other.

IMF - The International Monetary Fund. Normally they issue loans to developing countries to aid them with infrastructure problems and to overcome debt issues. Quite why taking on debt is a solution to debt problems is anyone's guess. Recently as part of the Troika, they have taken to bailing out western nations run by idiots.

Inflation - It is an increase in prices and a fall in the purchasing value of money. Meaning, prices go up and you are able to buy less with the money you have.

Glossary

Junk - Junk status or junk bonds all refer to economies getting so bad that they are basically equivalent to trash. A junk bond is rated below investment grade at the time of purchase. Investors are tempted to go after them (because they are insane) since they pay higher dividends due to them being very high risk. Junk status for a country is exactly the same thing. A country with junk status is a country very close to defaulting on its debt.

Merger - When two companies agree to join together and operate as one company, though possibly while still seeming to trade as two as before. Normally this means the rich get richer and more poor people are needed to work low paid jobs to keep them rich.

Nationalisation - When a government takes over a company and runs it. In the context of the crisis and banks, this exposes the national treasury to any debts the bank had. The Latin American version of this normally happens without the owner being paid, and a lot of rhetoric about how they were capitalist dogs.

PIIGS - This is a mean acronym to refer to a few countries in the European Union who are not doing as well as they should be compared to other European countries. These countries are Portugal, Ireland, Italy, Greece and Spain. It might be considered a derogatory term.

Property Bubble - Also known as a real estate bubble. This is when the housing market sees rapid increases in prices to unsustainable levels, before they crash back down again. These situations are almost always made worse by construction companies betting everything they have on trying to keep them going.

Rating Agency - The scourge of the financial world, ratings agencies are companies that research and analyse corporate and municipal bond issues and preferred stocks in an effort to assess their creditworthiness and the likelihood that investors will receive their payment. Recently they have been under scrutiny by countries and their citizens, as their evaluation can make or break an economy. If they say you can't pay your bills no one will lend you money and your interest rates will go up.

Troikapocalypse

Recession - A recession is the slowdown of an economic activity, generally signaled by a widespread drop in spending, a period of economic decline where industrial and trade activities are reduced. Officially it's marked by the fall of a country's Gross Domestic Product for two quarters or more in a row. Socially it's marked by an increase in unemployment, social instability and arguments over whose fault it is.

Securitised Mortgages - This is when banks group a lot of financial contracts together, for example 10,000 mortgages, and sell it on as a bond. The idea is that the bank gets money now, and the payments on the mortgages pay the repayments. If the mortgages don't get paid, the bank is then on the hook for the repayments. an especially clever idea when done with sub prime loans.

Sovereign Debt - It's what sovereign states owe to either national lenders (internal debt) or international lenders (external debt). Governments usually borrow by issuing products like securities, government bonds or bills. Meaning, pretend money. Like on Monopoly.

Sovereign Default - When a government cannot pay back its lenders that is called defaulting, this is what we call a sovereign default. It's what everyone is fearing that could happen in the European Union with a few of its states.

Stimulus Package - An attempt to stimulate economic growth by handing out a load of money to a load of people for a load of often crazy things.

Sub Prime Loan - A mortgage or loan given to a person or company who is a large risk. for example people with low income and/or a bad credit history. These loans normally have significantly worse terms. These are often bundled together and sold as securitised mortgages. essentially the predatory side of your friendly local bank showing how the poor get taken advantage of.

Subsidiary - A company that is is owned or controlled by another company. Normally useful for tax reasons or insulating the parent

Glossary

company from all the people who want to sue the subsidiary over their evil ways.

Tax Evasion - When people don't pay the tax they owe, or make it look like they owe less than they actually do. The national Greek sport.

Troika - The tripartite committee led by the European Commission with the European Central Bank and the International Monetary Fund, that organised loans to the governments of Greece, Ireland and Portugal, along with a few other countries. The Troika representatives monitor these countries' economies very closely, along with issuing advisories and recommendations to try to get these countries not to default and bring the European Union down with them.

Unemployment - This is an easy one, and very important. It is the state of NOT having a job. On a national scale, the percentage of the population that is without employment It is an important indicator of a healthy economy.

www.ingramcontent.com/pod-product-compliance
Lightning Source LLC
Chambersburg PA
CBHW032000170526
45157CB00002B/478